"To date or not to date, that is the question. Jessie answers it and a lot of others as she moves you from being 'crushed' to courageous in how you approach your love life."

DANNAH GRESH
bestselling author and creator, *Secret Keeper Girl*

"If you're devastated over a breakup—or know someone who is—this book is for you! Jessie is the real thing. You can trust her because she really does know about life—and love—and God—and she really does care about what you are going through. Cuddle up with this book and listen in as Jessie shares gobs of helpful stuff that really will make a difference in how you view yourself and guys."

ELISA MORGAN
speaker, author of *The Beauty of Broken*

"In a world that speaks lies to women, Crushed is full of truth about relationships and how to trust God with your love life. I wish I would have had a book like this when I was in my early teens! This book digs deep into real issues girls face and how to align our hearts to make God our number one love. A must-read for girls of any age!"

CARMEN JUSTICE
1 Girl Nation

"'God is enough.' This overarching theme ripples through this beautiful book in ways that inspire courage, hope, commitment, and grace. *Crushed* is honest, practical, realistic, and relevant. It challenges the lies of our current culture with God's compelling truth and awesome love. *Crushed* is both preventative and restorative. It is truth in unvarnished and engaging beauty. When God is enough, then we are free to follow His lead, His timing, His plan."

DAN WOLGEMUTH
President/CEO Youth For Christ, USA

WHY GUYS *DON'T* HAVE TO MAKE OR BREAK YOU

Life, Love & God Series

JESSIE MINASSIAN

CRUSHED

A THINK resource published by NavPress
in alliance with Tyndale House Publishers, Inc.

NAVPRESS ●.

NavPress is the publishing ministry of The Navigators, an international Christian organization and leader in personal spiritual development. NavPress is committed to helping people grow spiritually and enjoy lives of meaning and hope through personal and group resources that are biblically rooted, culturally relevant, and highly practical.

For more information, go to www.NavPress.com.

© 2014 by Jessie Minassian

A NavPress published resource in alliance with Tyndale House Publishers.

ISBN 978-1-61291-627-9

Published in association with the literary agency of Wolgemuth & Associates, Inc.

Some of the anecdotal illustrations in this book are true to life and are included with the permission of the persons involved. All other illustrations are composites of real situations, and any resemblance to people living or dead is coincidental.

Cataloging-in-Publication Data is Available.

Printed in the United States of America

19	18	17	16	15	14
8	7	6	5	2	1

To my heavenly Groom, who is enough for me.
And to the man of my dreams, Paul Daniel Minassian.
Thank you for choosing me.
Thank you for cherishing me.

Contents

Introduction

I've read a lot of books—*lots* of them—and all my favorites have something in common. Each one made me feel as if I were talking with a friend, or at least someone who cared about my life. I guess when it comes down to it, I don't like having someone I've never met tell me how to live. Wild guess here—maybe you don't either? It's easier to listen to advice when we hear it from someone we know and who we know cares about us, right? (And, let's be honest, sometimes it's really encouraging to hear that an author is *human*, just like the rest of us!) So before we dig into this book together, it's only fair that we get to know each other a bit.

I'm Jessie. My given name is actually Jessica, and my last name is so hard to pronounce that I avoid using it when possible. (Just for kicks, it's pronounced min-'a-see-in.) My single momma brought me into this world on a beautiful Californian March day just a *few* years ago (wink). She got married when I was five, and I grew up in a blended family of five kids. I played lots of sports in school and tried to figure out how to love God with my whole heart when it seemed to be *way* more interested in boys. (Maybe you can relate?) I liked school when I had friends, thought it was miserable when I didn't. I got good grades, ate too many Twix for lunch, and never got used to spending ten to twelve hours a week on a school bus. (We kind of lived in the boondocks.)

After high school graduation, I went to a Christian college in Southern California. I played volleyball there and then got into rock climbing. I studied abroad two semesters, one in Israel and the other in Costa Rica. I still liked school when I had friends and learned not to be miserable when I didn't. I got fewer good grades, stopped eating Twix for lunch, and traded the school bus for my first car (a ridiculously small, gold Toyota MR2). There were ups, there were downs, and then there was *him*.

I married my match made in heaven the weekend after college graduation. For now, let me just say that Paul (or "Paco," as most people know him) swept me off my feet and I have never looked back. Best friends make the best soul mates, and he was—and is—both. (*Awww!*) I didn't think I had room for any more love in my heart until God gave us two daughters, Ryan and Logan. They're sweet lil' blessings wrapped in two feisty packages!

Besides loving on my family, my greatest joy these days is to help girls find their identity, pleasure, and purpose in God. I'm the resident big sis for a website called LifeLoveandGod.com, where I answer girls' questions about, well, life, love, and God. (I know, pretty creative, right?) Now that I have two daughters of my own, I'm all the more passionate about seeing girls understand their unique beauty, know how amazing God is, and hold their heads high in dignity.

That's where the LIFE, LOVE AND GOD series comes in. These

books are meant to be the closest thing to just hanging out at my house, going for a hike together, or meeting for a small group in my living room. Each book covers different stuff you're facing, whether it's body image issues, the quest for identity, shameful addictions, or relationships with guys.

You'll want to have a notebook or journal handy for the discussion questions at the end of each chapter. Trust me, you'll get so much more out of this book if you take time to think through those questions. Even better if you can grab a couple of friends (or your mom or a youth group leader) and go through the book together! My heart is to see you grow in your relationship with God and shine with confidence, and that happens most often when you're in community with others.

You can find out more about my random favorite things on the "Meet Jessie" page at LifeLoveandGod.com. I'd love to hear a little about you, too, if you'd like to send me an e-mail at the website!

Now, without further ado, let's get talking about the real reason you picked up this book: guys.

Love,

jessie.

Part I

HAVE YOU BEEN CRUSHED?

CHAPTER 1

Those Blasted Butterflies

It all started my second-grade year. His name was Carlos.

I knew virtually nothing about him, other than that he was a really good tetherball player and liked to keep his dark hair high and tight. But he had dimples. The dimples are what did me in. My elementary school–aged heart was all aflutter while I waited in line to play tetherball at recess. I was actually glad when he broke his arm because it meant I got to sign his cast. (How twisted is that?) I noticed whenever he got up to sharpen his pencil, and when his name wasn't called during attendance, I was sincerely disappointed. I don't remember him ever speaking, actually, let alone talking to me. Come to think of it, he may not have known English. But his silence didn't deter me. I was smitten.

Ridiculous, I know. But even more ridiculous is that it didn't end in the second grade. After Carlos came Jordan and Ronnie, Cody and John, Chad, Mirage, Randy, Jake . . . the list goes on and on. We're talking double-digit crushes before I even got to high school. It's not pretty.

I didn't know it then, but I was a budding crushaholic. *What's a crushaholic?* you might ask. Great question. Other than it being a word I completely made up (you'll find I tend to do that), a crushaholic is someone who can't seem to go for more than a couple of months, weeks, or maybe even *days* without having romantic feelings for someone. And most girls born in the past quarter century seem to fit into this category. Whether falling for a friend from school or smitten with a Hollywood hottie, a crushaholic has a hard time not having a "like" in her life. And those likes usually translate into boyfriends whenever the object of her affection actually likes her back.

To be honest, I went through most of my life not realizing the permanent damage being done to my heart by all those likes and, eventually, relationships. At the time, it seemed so natural and unavoidable to like someone—kind of like breathing, or dying, or blushing when you realize you've just said something completely idiotic. It may have seemed unavoidable and natural, but now I know better. And I hope I can help you see a better way too.

The truth is our crushes are *crushing* us. We're letting our relationship status define our identities. We're letting guys and society tell us who we should be, and we're bending over backward to become what we think some guy will want. And the weight of all our flitting affections, the broken hearts, jealousy, breakups, betrayals, and let-downs, the longing for someone we can't have, and the scars left from having relationships we shouldn't be in—they're taking a toll.

We're being crushed by the weight of our own affections.

The dating-go-round—the cycle of crush, date, break up, crush on someone else—that seems so natural in our society ends up crippling us emotionally. Unless you break free and are willing to challenge the dating "norm," your heart may be pretty mangled by the time you give it to the man God has for you to marry someday. (Or, if you don't get married, the dating-go-round could leave you with a broken, bitter heart for a companion.) Even more devastating, all the crushes and dysfunctional relationships with guys are stealing our hearts from the One who should be the center of our lives now, today, in this moment.

The good news is there's a better way. That's what this book is all about: finding out that God has given us a way to love that doesn't include letting guys make or break us. The God who made you and delights in you wants more for you than to rise and fall with each passing relationship. *I* want more for you than that! I'm sure you do too.

I hope you'll be willing to discover that "better way" together by digging into God's Word and taking some time to get to the, ahem, *heart* of the matter in your own life. My hope for you, as we walk through these pages together, is that you'll find out who you are and how to find contentment in who God is. I hope you'll dream with me about what kind of relationship you want to have someday and figure out a game plan to glorify God with your life in the meantime. And I hope you'll find that it *is*, in fact, possible to make it through life without getting your heart crushed by the weight of your own affections and relationships with those (mighty fine) members of the opposite sex.

Profile of a Crush

At the risk of sounding painfully elementary, let's tackle first things first: What is a crush, anyway?

The more I've thought about that word, the more curious it sounds. The dictionary defines *crush* primarily in terms of "pound," "destroy," and "oppress." (Ironic, huh? Not that any of us have ever felt pounded by emotions, destroyed by rejection, or oppressed by other girls who like the same guy, right?) Nope, the puppy love variety of *crush* gets just one out of nine definitions for the word.

> **crush** \ˈkrəsh\ *noun* : an intense and usually passing infatuation; also : the object of infatuation.[1]

If I could be so bold as to challenge the sacred tome of wisdom also known as *Webster's*, I'd expect to see a little more ink given to this great plight of young adulthood. I mean, come on now—that's it? What about the butterflies, longing, and sometimes all-around obsession for someone who may or may not know you exist? Show a little empathy, Webby! Besides, I don't know how "passing" most crushes are. Some can last years. But there you have it: the crush. It doesn't matter if you're six or sixty—the chance of being pounded, destroyed, and oppressed by bashful blue eyes seems to remain the same.

Most people will tell you that crushes aren't dangerous. They're pretty much expected from girls as young as elementary school. Our favorite TV stars have them, our big sisters have them, our BFFs have them. "Liking" someone is almost a rite of passage in our culture these days—just part of growing up—kind of like pimples, tampons, and a high school diploma. And why not? Crushes are harmless, right?

I wish they were. Really, I do. The butterflies and hoping and dreaming and scheming can be fun! But after thirteen years of flitting from crush to crush before I wised up, I'm here to tell you that a crush (and especially a crush addiction) can come with serious side effects.

But what's so dangerous about having a crush? To answer that question, we're going to have to ask another one first.

Queens of Hearts

Let me ask you this: What makes us have those crush feelings for guys? Why do we get the butterflies, the sweaty palms, the "please-oh-please notice me" rush of emotions?

Obviously, God made girls and guys to like each other—to be attracted to the opposite sex. (It helps with that whole "be fruitful and multiply" command.) But if you were to go to a guy's slumber party (not that they'd ever call it that), you'd hear a lot less talk about who likes who and a whole lot more talk about the latest first-person shooter game. Why do girls specifically want relationships so badly? Why are we the ones who read romance novels, watch romantic comedies, and dream about romantic walks on the beach? Why can we girls be so obsessed with love and relationships?

I think there are two reasons. First, part of our love for romance is how God made us as girls—how He wired us.

Genesis 1:27 says that God made both man and woman "in his own image." Men and women both bear some parts of His image, such as His creativity and desire for justice. But He also split some of His image between the two of them. God gave some of His qualities primarily to Adam (that is, those qualities we call "masculine," such as strength and steadiness) and some of His qualities to Eve (think "feminine" qualities like gentleness and beauty). To put it another way, Adam plus

Eve equaled the complete image of God, or as close as a human pair could come to it. When Adam chose Eve and they became one flesh, they became a more complete human replica of the whole image of God.

One of those qualities God gave primarily to Eve—one of His divine characteristics in human form—is a love for romance. (If you've ever read Isaiah, you've heard firsthand the romantic language God uses to describe the love He has for His chosen people.) In fact, the Bible says that God *is* love (see 1 John 4:8). And even though guys definitely feel and show love in their own ways, we girls have an uncanny knack for romance. The feeling of excitement and mystery associated with love comes more naturally to us, in general at least. It's just the way God made us.

But there's a second reason girls delight in romance more than guys, and it also goes back to the garden.

I Want You to Want Me

God wanted Adam and Eve to fit perfectly—heart, body, and soul—so He gave girls and guys different roles to play in romance. God knew that Adam and Eve's relationship would work best if they were like two pieces of a puzzle: equal in worth, but different in design. These two pieces, when joined, would fit together like chocolate and coconut, rainbows and dark clouds, tall boots and skinny jeans. So God gave Adam a desire to pursue Eve, to chase and win her. And (here's our part) God gave us a desire to be desired. God preprogrammed each girl to be the one pursued, the one treasured and sought after. We want to be wanted. And that's not a bad thing! (It was part of God's design, remember.) But we have to understand the nature of our desire if we're not going to be owned by it, because that innocent and pure desire to be desired by a man got warped when sin entered the picture.

When both Adam and Eve were operating under God's will and keeping His rules, things were peachy. Adam found his worth in God, pursued Eve, cared for her, and treated her with the honor she deserved. Eve also found her worth in God, was her beautiful self, helped Adam around the garden, respected him, and delighted in his love. They fit. And they were both truly happy.

Then came sin.

I'm sure you know the story. Satan, God's mortal enemy, disguised himself as a snake and got to work deceiving Eve. Satan promised Eve that if she ate the fruit God had forbidden her to eat, she'd "be like God, knowing both good and evil" (Genesis 3:5). And Eve bought the lie hook, line, and sinker. She ate the fruit, disobeying God's clear instructions, and then gave some to Adam to eat. He followed suit, and the rest is a sad human history of sin, pain, regret, and rage against God.

But what does this have to do with a girl's desire to be desired? Well, when Adam and Eve sinned, they received the consequences that went along with disobeying God. Adam's and Eve's roles in their relationship didn't fit as flawlessly anymore. Because of sin, Adam stopped being perfect, and so did Eve. Their stubborn wills began to clash. Adam didn't always pursue or care for Eve or treat her with the honor she deserved. Eve was no longer content "just" to help Adam, doubted her beauty, and had trouble respecting him. And because of the curse, instead of delighting in Adam's love, Eve battled to rule over him. They didn't fit perfectly anymore because sin came between them.

God created us to love and be loved, but our obsession with romance was never His design. Our obsession with being wanted—our over-the-top desire to be desired—is a backlash from the curse. Because of sin, we're not content to wait for love until God's timing; we'd rather take matters into our own hands. God told Eve that because of her sin, "[she would] desire to control [her] husband" (Genesis 3:16). That desire to control creates all sorts of chaos in marriage, but I think it's pretty obvious that it messes things up way before that.

Think about it. Have you ever tried to control a guy's feelings for you? Have you ever dressed to impress a guy, flirted to get his attention, or tried to control the way he acts toward you or others? Is God enough for you, or do you feel you need a boyfriend to be happy? Are you willing to wait for a guy to pursue you—to lead you, the way God designed—or are you set on taking matters into your own hands just to get what you want? (We're going to talk more about a guy's role as leader in chapter 6.)

Our culture hardly helps with this. We're told as girls that we can do anything and be anything and shouldn't let anything stop us from getting what we want. (Don't get me wrong; I completely believe that women are capable and strong and have the same rights as men. But we can't forget that God gave men and women different roles on purpose, for our benefit.) When the curse of sin and the bullhorn of society get together, the sound can be enough to bust our eardrums. We're being told that we're failing as girls if we're not getting our way. Just like in the garden, Satan is hissing in our ears, "You deserve to have that guy like you. Just go get him. Tell him how you feel. Do whatever it takes to make him yours. A guy will make you happier than God ever could."

I get so stinkin' mad when I think about the way Satan twists the truth to deceive us, because when we live our lives God's way, there's so much peace and joy—and hope! But when we listen to Satan's lies, everything gets twisted. We end up confused and hurt and messed up.

I know you want to be wanted by a guy. So do I! All of us girls have a desire to be desired. That's the way God made us. We just can't let that God-given desire get twisted up in Satan's lies. We can't let him convince us we *have* to be in a relationship to be complete and happy and have a full and delicious life.

So what do we do with those feelings? How can we want to be wanted without becoming obsessed with guys and relationships? To start with, we'll have to get control of our thought life.

Taming the Wilds

We girls are pretty much notorious for how easily we fall for guys. Humor me for a sec and envision this scene with me. . . .

You walk into church and take your seat with your usual group of friends in the fourth row back from the front. Just before the worship band gets up to play, you notice something out of place in the front row—something beautifully, mysteriously, *gorgeously* out of place. "Who's *that*?!" you whisper to your friend on your left, pointing to the hotness who has just turned to shake hands with the pastor. Friend doesn't know, but you're not left wondering for long. The pastor takes the stage and introduces him as a guest worship leader for the morning. His name is Benji Lemberg.

Helloooo, Benji Lemberg, you think to yourself.

The first song begins, but you're not really thinking about the words you're singing. (Something about God being everything, yada yada . . .) You're a little preoccupied with the sandy-blond hair hanging so perfectly over one of Benji's eyes. There's something about a cute guy . . . with a guitar . . . singing worship . . . that makes a girl forget all reason. *He's perfect*, you find yourself thinking. *He even loves God!* Before the first song is over, you've imagined him asking you out. By the end of worship, he's taking you to a romantic dinner. By the end of the pastor's message, Benj (as you now like to call him) has proposed and you're Mrs. Lemberg and you have three kids, a dog, and a beach house, all in your sweet little mind.

Sound familiar? (It does to me. Okay, so maybe that's another true and embarrassing story.)

What is it about us that causes us to fall head over heels for someone we barely know? Maybe you don't fall for guys quite as quickly as I did, but have you ever had feelings for someone you knew crazy little about? Strangely, it seems the less we know about a guy, the easier it is for us to crush on him. Maybe it's because, in the absence of the details about him, we get to fill in the blanks with our imagination. When he's new, or quiet, or shy, we can make him whoever we would *like* him to be. We think the perfect guy into existence, and right away our feelings for him start ramping up.

Here's the point: Our feelings, including "crush" feelings, come from the thoughts we think. This truth can revolutionize so many areas of our lives! So I'm going to say it again: Our feelings come from our thoughts. Goodness knows we girls have trouble with all *kinds* of emotions. Sheesh! If we can get to the root of them—if we can pinpoint which lies we're believing and think true thoughts instead—our emotions, and our lives, will be so much healthier.

Philippians 4:8-9 says,

> Fix your thoughts on what is true, and honorable, and right, and pure, and lovely, and admirable. Think about things that are excellent and worthy of praise. . . . Then the God of peace will be with you.

If we live these verses, we can, in fact, tame the wilds of our thought life, which will bring our emotions right in line (that's the "peace" part).

Here's what I mean:

If I think . . .	Then I'll feel . . .
Only two weeks till summer break!	Relief, excitement, anticipation
Aye-chi-mama—he's a hottie-tottie with a rockin' body!	Desire, longing
I'm the only single girl on the planet.	Loneliness, isolation
Guys never notice me. Something must be wrong with me.	Discontentment, self-loathing
I'm beautiful just the way I am.	Confidence, peace
I don't have to be in a relationship to be complete. God is enough for me!	Contentment, hope, joy

Does that make sense? I'm not trying to offer you some simple, three-step, "positive thinking" solution to all your problems. I can't even promise that *all* your emotions will behave once you start thinking true thoughts! But I do know that you are called to "let God transform you into a new person by changing the way you think. Then you will learn to know God's will for you, which is good and pleasing and perfect" (Romans 12:2). If we'll let God transform our way of thinking from boy-centered thoughts to true, honorable, right, pure, lovely, and admirable thoughts, we can break the crush cycle. I'm not saying you'll never have feelings for a guy ever again (who would want that?). But you won't be ruled by those emotions, and you won't obsess over guys, which will be super important as we move through the next few chapters.

After we get control of our thoughts, the second way we can "desire to be desired" without becoming obsessed with guys and relationships is to understand the difference between attraction and admiration.

Attraction or Admiration?

I'm about to share a truth with you that I wish I had understood back in second grade. I honestly think it would have revolutionized my love life and freed me from the cycle of crushes and bad relationships that plagued most of my growing-up years. I hope you'll take it to heart: There's a difference between attraction and admiration.

Remember how, when God made Adam and Eve, He gave certain qualities primarily to Adam and certain qualities primarily to Eve? How He designed them to be two pieces of a puzzle that joined perfectly together? Well, it just so happens that He also gave us an admiration for the qualities He gave to the opposite sex. As girls, we're drawn to the masculine qualities God gave Adam—not only his masculine body, but also his strength, steadiness, confidence, and desires to conquer, protect, and be tender toward a woman. Guys too are drawn to the feminine qualities God gave us as girls—not only our beautiful bodies,[2] but also our gentleness, sensitivity, care for others, and desire to nurture and support.

As girls, we're drawn to those masculine qualities and other characteristics like faith, a sense of humor, and caring for others. We're wired to admire those things. The problem comes when we mistake that admiration for being attracted romantically to that person. In my true confession about Benji Lemberg earlier, I admired his looks, sure, but also his musicality, his confidence, and the way he seemed to love God and others. But I took it too far; I let that admiration confuse me. Just because you admire someone doesn't mean you like him romantically or *have to* like him in that way. Going back to taming the wilds of our thought life, here are two ways I could have handled that particular situation:

Focus on Attraction		Focus on Admiration	
Thoughts	*Emotions*	*Thoughts*	*Emotions*
Who's THAT? My good-ness. God sure did a good job on that one!	Desire	He's a good-looking guy.	Admiration
He's so spiritual. He'd make a great boyfriend.	More desire	I think I'd like to wait for a guy who loves God enough to pro-claim Him in public.	Hope for the future
I can just imagine us together. We'd be like . . . the PERFECT couple.	Even more desire	God, help me become the kind of girl who will make a good partner for a guy like that someday.	Trust (in God)

Do you see the difference? We have a choice about whether we'll take Philippians 4:8-9 to heart and keep the wilds of our thought life under control. We can choose whether to think thoughts that will keep our admiration from flaring up into full-blown attraction.

The power to crush (or not to crush) is ultimately in your hands with God's help, my friend. And that's really good news because if you do find a wonderful man someday and the two of you get married, there's no off switch to that admiration you'll have for masculinity. You don't just wake up one morning as a newlywed and find you no longer admire masculine qualities like good looks, confidence, and strength in other members of the opposite sex. If it weren't possible to keep your admiration from turning into full-out attraction, even married women would be falling for every manly man out there! (Unfortunately, many married men and women *still* don't understand the difference between admiration and attraction and how to control their thoughts. Hence, the divorce rate, right?)

Is having a crush on someone wrong? Of course not. But it's not necessarily healthy, either. And it's not always harmless. It's the warped thinking behind our crushes that's dangerous, like telling ourselves he's perfect for us when we barely know him, convincing ourselves we *have* to be in a relationship with him to be happy, and confusing admiration for attraction. When our thinking about guys and relationships (and God, for that matter) is off, one crush quickly becomes two . . . then three . . . then a bunch . . . and a cycle is born.

The crush cycle is dangerous. We're going to talk more about why in the next chapter. But at least for now you're armed with some tools to help you battle those butterflies as you learn to admire your male counterparts without losing your head. You are stronger than your emotions!

Will you pray with me?

God of the Universe, everything You make is good, including guys and girls and emotions and romance. Help me to understand my own heart and make sense of my emotions.

Show me any sinful thoughts I'm letting run wild in my mind, and give me the discipline to tame them. Please, Lord, make me a new person by changing the way I think about everything in life, including guys and love and dating. I want to bring You glory in every aspect of my life, including my love life. Amen.

Discussion Questions

1. *Try to count up the number of crushes you've had in the past few years. What does that number tell you about the state of your heart?*

2. *What are the two reasons girls "desire to be desired" by a guy?*

3. *Do you struggle to keep your thought life under control? How do those thoughts affect your emotions?*

4. *If unhelpful or unhealthy thoughts about guys get you in trouble, where can you "fix your thoughts" instead?*

5. What's the difference between admiring a member of the opposite sex and being attracted to him?

6. What do you think? Are crushes harmless, or do they affect our hearts in any negative ways? Why or how?

7. Take out that journal we talked about in the introduction and spend a few minutes writing about how the feelings you've had for guys have affected your life. What do you think it would be like not to have a crush on someone for a while? Do you think it's possible?

CHAPTER 2

He Can't Make You Whole

By the time I graduated from college, my passport was stamped in Fiji, Egypt, Ukraine, Australia, Czech Republic, Costa Rica, and seven other countries. I guess you could say I had the travel bug. Studying and traveling outside the United States opened my eyes to cultures, customs, people, and places I had only read about in books. It's one thing to hear your parents tell you to eat your food because there are children starving in Africa (eye-roll excused); it's a totally different ball game to see a starved, dirty-faced child, dressed in rags, hands held palms up, begging you for something . . . *anything*. And it's one thing to read the second commandment, "You must not make for yourself an idol of any kind" (Exodus 20:4), but quite another to smell the thick smoke of incense at a stone shrine in Guatemala or to see the brightly painted plastic and wooden family idols lined on shelves in a corner of a room in Cuba. When you see solemn faces bowed in prayer to these gods that couldn't help a spider catch a fly—well, I guess God says it best:

> How foolish are those who manufacture idols. These prized objects are really worthless. . . . Who but a fool would make his own god—an idol that cannot help him one bit? (ISAIAH 44:9-10)

God goes on to say in verses 11-20 exactly what all of us are thinking: Who in his right mind would think that some object a person made could possess the powers of the true God?

Here's a modern picture of Isaiah 44. Let's say I went out back one day and chopped down my maple tree. I could throw half the wood in the fireplace to keep warm on a cozy winter night. But let's say that I'd whittle down the other half to resemble a life-size Elvis. I might even paint it with some sparkly acrylic paints and make that signature hairdo with a wig from Walmart. And let's not forget the classic suit made of white leather and gold piping. Once my personal Elvis looked as if he were ready to sing "Jailhouse Rock," I'd prop him up in a corner of my living room, make sure he was nice and comfy, and then kneel down and pray to my king of rock.

That's ridiculous, right?

Can I be honest with you? I admit that for a good part of my life when I read passages like Isaiah 44, I felt a swelling sense of pride. *Sheesh, those people are idiots! Who would be so blockheaded that they'd think those idols are real? I'm glad I'm not that stupid, God. But really, who would do that?* Just being honest. And I'm really glad God is so patient with our own sin because, come to find out, *I* was one of those idiots who trusted in something that couldn't save me. I was guilty of worshipping something made by someone else, expecting it to do something it could never do. Although the objects of my affections were tons better-looking than my homemade Elvis, they had a lot in common.

According to the principles in Isaiah 44, an idol is anything (1) made that (2) takes God's rightful place as the number one priority in my life.

By that definition, aren't we guilty of letting all *sorts* of idols take over our hearts? Everything (music, social media, clothes, sports) can take on idol status if we're not careful. God knows how quickly we replace Him with just about anything and everything. That's why He dedicated not just one but two of the Ten Commandments to warn us against idolatry:

> You must not have any other god but me. . . . You must not bow down to them or worship them, for I, the LORD your God, am a jealous God who will not tolerate your affection for any other gods. (EXODUS 20:3,5)

The word *affection* is what gives away most girls' number one idol. C'mon now, you don't have to ace calculus to see the connection. We, my friend, idolize guys. They fit both criteria. They're made (by God—and we're very thankful, Lord!). And they easily—*so* easily—take the number one spot in our affections, time, energy, hopes, dreams, focus, conversations (need I go on?). In a nutshell, when we allow guys to monopolize our hearts, we're already worshipping *them*, not God. It doesn't matter if a guy is a crush, your husband, or anything in between. No guy—not even "Mr. Right"—should take God's rightful place in your life.

When we allow guys to become our centers, when we let them "make us," then they can, and will most certainly, break us. I'm not saying most guys would hurt us on purpose, but worshipping guys is not what God intended for us. And just as Eve learned, when we try to do things our own way, it gets ugly real fast! God made Adam and Eve to reflect His character together and bring Himself glory. God made them to enjoy one another's love, sure, but He never intended for them to be consumed with one another. That sad and destructive aspect of human love came only after sin entered the picture.

What Can You Do for Me?

The reason those people I saw in Cuba and Guatemala (and many other places around the world) worship idols is they're hoping the deities they represent will do something for them. Maybe they're asking for rain or protection from evil spirits or healing for a loved one. Only the true God can do those things. Gut-check time: Are we any different? When we worship a guy, a relationship, or the thought of marriage, aren't we trusting that six-foot, blue-eyed cutie to do something only the true and living God can do for us?

But what exactly are we hoping a guy will do? Why are we so drawn to worshipping something *made* instead of the God who made us? Romans 1:25 gives us the answer:

> They traded the truth about God for a lie. So they worshiped and served the things God created instead of the Creator himself, who is worthy of eternal praise!

Why do we idolize guys? Because we've traded the truth about God for a lie—or, in this case, for *four* lies. We worship "the [guys] God created instead of the Creator himself" because we're blind enough to think guys can do what only God can.

Lie #1: He'll prove I'm beautiful and desired.

In chapter 1, we talked a lot about that God-given ache of ours to be desired. As girls, we want to be wanted. Part of that is just our God-given design. Originally, Eve's desire to be desired was soothed by the One who made her. She knew she must have been wanted; God didn't have to make her, but He did. God *wanted* to make Eve, for His glory and for Adam's good. But once sin entered the picture, Eve began to doubt everything. And you know what they say: The apple doesn't fall far from the tree. Now, as Eve's daughters, we doubt our worth and we doubt God's love; we doubt our beauty and we doubt our desirability.

Because of the Fall—because sin made us far from God—our desire to be desired got supersized. And just like we hope that extra-large order of fries will somehow magically hit the spot, we think we'll scratch that itch to feel desirable if we have guys in our lives.

Have you ever felt that way? Doesn't it seem—at least sometimes—that if you just had a special someone to call you "his," then you'd *know* you were beautiful? You'd *know* you were wanted? Are you convinced that if you could have a solid relationship with a guy who really loved you, you wouldn't need anything else? Hmmm. Wouldn't need *anything* else. That's the lie, isn't it? Once again we're trying to fill the God-shaped hole in our hearts with something other than God: an idol.

Let me share a thing or two about what God has already said about your worth, beauty, and desirability; then you tell me if you think that should be enough for us or whether we should also need a guy's approval to have value.

My dear sister, what are you worth? You are worth the price of the King of the Universe. Your heart is so precious to Him that He was willing to move heaven and earth to claim it. God wants a relationship with you so badly that He allowed His only, precious Son, Jesus, to die a brutal and unfair death to make it possible for you to be together with Him always—for eternity! If you belong to Jesus, you are part of the church, and He calls you His bride. Would the King of kings get engaged to trash? I think not.

How beautiful are you? God says you were meticulously and purposefully made from head to foot to bring Him glory, not so you could wallow in your perceived imperfections or get all high on yourself as if you made yourself beautiful. And God delights in you so much that He *sings* over you! That's pretty incredible![3]

So, is that enough? Is what God says about you—what He's done for you—all the praise you need? Do you live like it's enough? Or are you too busy trying to catch that cute guy's attention or too wrapped up in a relationship to remember God's truth?

Can I ask you something? Do you know this God? Have you ever truly, completely given your heart to the God who spoke the universe into being with a word, yet so sweetly calls to you? If you haven't, then please don't go any further without making things right between the two of you. Turning from death to life is surprisingly not complicated! Romans 10:9 says,

If you openly declare that Jesus is Lord and believe in your heart that God raised him from the dead, you will be saved.

Because of our sin, we're separated from God; because Jesus died on the cross for our sins, things can be made right with Him again. All we have to do is admit our sinfulness and then stop running away from God and run *to* Him instead! That means we have to be willing to follow His way of life, and we have to be willing to start believing His truth instead of the lies we've believed up to this point. But the rewards of a relationship with the living God way outshine the things you'll give up. Trust me![4]

Speaking of lies, let's look at a few more together.

Lie #2: He'll end my loneliness forever.

Ever felt lonely? Yeah, me too. And we live in the age of supposed connection, right? I mean, you could be completely alone in a room, but if you have your computer or tablet or smartphone with you, you're instantly connected to millions of people all over the world (theoretically, at least). But we're no less lonely than any other generation in history. In fact, some experts argue that we're actually lonelier now than ever before.

Not that feeling lonely is a new thing. Even King David (some three thousand years ago) wrote often about feeling alone. Here's a guy God called a man after His own heart, yet he admits, "I lie awake, lonely as a solitary bird on the roof" (Psalm 102:7). His son Solomon, the wisest man to ever live, also admitted that even when hanging out with a group of happy people, one can *still* feel lonely sometimes. He said,

"Laughter can conceal a heavy heart, but when the laughter ends, the grief remains" (Proverbs 14:13).

Feeling lonely is a part of life. We've all been there at times (some more than others!). When we don't feel wanted, connected, or understood, it's so tempting to turn to our idols instead of to God. We want the pain to stop, like *yesterday*, so we reach for a quick fix—a flesh-and-blood person (or drugs, cutting, alcohol, shopping, or anything else that will immediately numb the pain). And having a guy in your life probably *will* end the loneliness for a time. But remember the limitations of idols? They can't do for you what only God can do. They can't change your heart. They can't fix the internal problem, so the loneliness will eventually return.

This totally reminds me of some stuff called Dermoplast. Have you ever heard of it? I was introduced to this little miracle in a bottle after getting stitches at the hospital. The nurse handed me a blue and white aerosol can and told me to spray it on the incredibly painful sutures. I tried it. Voilà! No more pain. I felt like I could dance a jig—for about thirty minutes. Then the pain returned, and I wanted to cry like a baby all over again! (Yeah, pain tolerance is not one of my strong suits.)

Just like that Dermoplast, an idol will most certainly feel good in the moment. It will numb the pain for a while. But would you rather have temporary relief from the loneliness, only to have it return in full force later? Or would you rather be healed? The amazing thing about God is that He is enough! The Bible says He is *Yahweh Rophe*, "the Lord who heals," and His Son, Jesus, is the great "Physician," *Iatros*. God is completely able to heal you—to fill you and complete you. I'm not saying that God will completely erase from your brain the ability to feel lonely, but I do believe that when your heart is feasting on Him instead of longing for a guy, that intense feeling of isolation will fade. It *is* possible to find your identity in God—to believe His truth instead of the lie that you have to be connected to a guy to be whole.

That's one of the things I love about David's brutal honesty in the Psalms: He always brought it back around to God's truth. He could vent up a storm—talk all about his enemies and how unfairly he was treated, how scared he was or how he was pretty sure he was steps away from death—but then turn right around and praise God for His faithfulness, goodness, love, mercy, and ability to save him from every freaky situation. David understood that his loneliness wasn't the end of the world because he was never truly alone. Sure, at the beginning of Psalm 102, he felt like a lonely little bird on a roof (see verse 7). He was crying so hard that his tears ran down his face into his cup (see verse 9). But by the end of the psalm, as he starts to recount the truth about who God is—that "he will appear in his glory" and "will listen to the prayers of the destitute" (verses 16-17)—David became confident that generations "[would] thrive in [God's] presence" (verse 28).

Some loneliness will always be a part of life, in different seasons and at different intensities. Will you trust that the God who made and adores you will be there for you during those times? I promise He's a much better comforter than even a pair of broad, male shoulders. If you want true peace, cling to the Maker, not the made.

Lie #3: He'll make me perfectly happy.

Flip open the latest girls' magazine and you'll see picture after picture of guys and girls together, laughing, touching, giving piggyback rides, holding hands, having picnics in the park, yada yada, sheesh. And—have you noticed?—they're always smiling. Commercials, billboards, Internet ads—they're all pretty much the same. If you judged reality by the media, having a significant other in your life *does* magically make the world a brighter, happier place. But is it true? Will being in a relationship make you happy?

Nope—at least, not in the long run.

This lie is really similar to the second one we just looked at ("He'll End My Loneliness Forever"). Just like we turn to guys to temporarily relieve our loneliness (like spraying Dermoplast on a cut), we often also turn to them to find happiness. Let's recap the truth: God did not make Adam and Eve to find their complete satisfaction in each other. We have God-shaped holes in the center of our hearts that only He can fill. Only God can fix what's gone terribly wrong because of sin. No guy—no matter how "perfect"—can do the trick.

The Bible gives us a glimpse at who is truly joyful:

- The girl who understands God's unfailing love—that He sees her troubles and cares about her deep pain (see Psalm 31:7)
- The girl who has been forgiven by God for everything she ever did and now lives in "complete honesty" (see Psalm 32:1-2)
- The girl who has Yahweh as her God (see Psalm 144:15)
- The girl who puts her hope in the God who made everything, not in idols (see Psalm 146:5-6)
- The girl who embraces God's wisdom and gains understanding (see Proverbs 3:13,18)

- The girl who has mercy on the poor (see Proverbs 14:21)
- The girl who trusts in the Lord and follows His instruction (see Proverbs 16:20; 29:18)

There's a deep joy that comes from being right with God, abiding with and living rightly before Him. I can't explain it, but it far outshines the "happiness" that comes from earthly relationships. It doesn't make human sense because it's a divine truth. Our hearts were made ultimately for God, to be filled by God's love and to return that love.

Now, here's the really cool part. (As if true, heartfelt joy wasn't enough!) When we *do* allow God to "make us"—make us whole, complete, valuable, connected, and joyful—then the more superficial feelings of happiness often follow too. Let's say that one day God does bring an amazing man into your life. If you've already allowed God to make you whole, a God-centered relationship with that man will be the icing on the cake of your happiness! And what's more, you won't be depending on that man to make you happy (which can destroy a marriage).

Let's imagine for a minute that my heart is like a bucket. If I'm empty, I'm going to be begging my significant other to fill me up. I'm going to feel insecure when he doesn't make me feel beautiful, and lonely when he's not around. I'll beg him for attention and manipulate his affections for me. Ugly, right? But if I've let Jesus (the Living Water) fill me up to the brim, any loving gestures my man pours in will only send my happiness overflowing, spilling out to refresh him and everyone else around me. Make sense? Let's find our true joy in God, not in some Hollywood version of happily ever after.

Lie #4: He'll end my single status for good.

Maybe it's the media onslaught of perfectly coupled, happy people we talked about earlier that started the stigma of being single. I don't know. But I do know, as I'm sure you do, that there seems to be a whole lot of focus on relationships everywhere you look. When you're constantly seeing (what seem to be) happy couples all around you, being single can feel like a fate worse than death (which it's not, obviously). I haven't forgotten how it feels to be the only single person in a group of friends, be solo on Valentine's Day, or show up to a prom or wedding without a date. It can be rough.

Singleness gets amplified when you're, well, single. And sometimes when we're flyin' solo, we can focus so hard on our single status that it gets somewhat blown out of proportion. We can easily forget that we are still whole human beings, capable of the same quality of life as our "taken" friends. And let's be honest, sometimes we can act just a little spoiled, pouting because we don't have what she has when we want it right now. The Bible has a more mature name for our modern-day Jonesing: coveting (which God warns against in the tenth commandment).

But let's take a step back here and look at the bigger picture. If you're single, let's just admit that it can be a rough place to be. I'd even call it a type of suffering. But will having a relationship with a guy right now guarantee that you'll never be single again? Quite the opposite is true. Here's a mind-bending thought for you: Every romantic relationship you have on this earth will end. Every single one. If you have a boyfriend now, there's a good chance you'll break up. If you get married, eventually one of you will die. Pessimistic? No, just realistic. There's a good chance you and I are both going to spend quite a bit of time in this life at a table for one. If we're not okay with singleness, we're going to spend that time fighting bitterness, envy, and discontentment. Put another way, we're going to be fighting against God.

Here's a hard truth, but I know you can handle it: You might be single your whole life. It's not like The Game of Life, where you get to put a little blue man in your car just for playing. God doesn't hand out husband tickets with our salvation. When we give Him the reins to our lives, we're giving up control—period. That's not a bad thing! God is all-knowing, all-powerful, all-wise, and all-good, and He promises to give us everything we need (see 2 Corinthians 9:8)—not want, but need. You can be confident that if a husband is what's best for your spiritual journey, God will bring your Prince Charming when the time is right. But if He knows that you will serve Him better in single-ness, like the apostle Paul talks about in 1 Corinthians 7, then single you'll stay. And that's no less of a blessing! Are you willing to trust God with everything, even your love life?

A relationship at this point in your life might temporarily end your "single status," true. But if it's not the right relation-ship at the right time (meaning the relationship God has chosen for you in His perfect timing), it's not going to be as fulfilling as you might hope. Like we talked about earlier, when we allow Jesus to fill our hearts to overflowing with His Living Water, then and only then can we enjoy the blessings of an earthly romance to the max.

So those are the lies. What do you think? Have you replaced God's truth with any of these four lies? Are you ready to believe that God is able to do for you what no guy possibly can?

Sweeter Than Honey (or Grapes)

A few years back, my husband, Paul, and I went to this gorgeous, little-known paradise called Havasu Falls in Arizona. You have to see it to believe how beautiful it is. Imagine five crystal-clear waterfalls cut into red rocks, falling dramatically into turquoise-blue pools. Think Maui crossed with the Grand Canyon and you get the idea. Paradise found! The only catch is that you can't drive there, or bike, or take a tourist tram. The only way in is on foot. The ten miles in wasn't so bad; it was the trip *out* that got me. Hiking ten miles with a thirty-pound pack is no walk in the park to begin with. Add to that a 2,400-foot elevation gain through a bone-dry, rocky canyon and you'll forgive me for feeling a little tired—and thirsty.

There's only one trail connecting the outside world to the Havasupai Indian village at the bottom of the canyon, so the villagers send pack mules up and down with mail, soda, toilet paper—you know, the important stuff. Well, the mule train that had come down a little while before we began our climb out just so happened to be carrying fruit. I love fruit. There must have been a small hole in one of the crates because every few feet along the trail, we saw a single green grape lying in the dirt.

At first it was funny to smoosh them with my hiking boots. But after a mile or so, I started getting really thirsty. Mind you, I'd eaten nothing but camp food and energy bars for a few days, and those green, plump, juicy grapes started getting all up in my head. Another mile farther on the trail I found myself thinking, *They don't really even look dirty. Maybe I'll try just one.* So I picked up a vegetarian roadkill, rinsed it off with my water bottle, and popped it into my mouth. *Hmmm . . . surprisingly refreshing*, I thought. Never mind my dear husband laughing at me—I was hooked.

For the last several miles of our hike out of Havasu, I quenched my thirst with dusty green grapes. Even admitting this on paper has me questioning my mental stability. I guess that's the point, though. I was so parched that I became irrational. I justified my actions because I was basically desperate.

There is a point to this embarrassing confession. It has to do with one of my favorite verses, tucked away near the end of the book of Proverbs:

> A person who is full refuses honey, but even bitter food
> tastes sweet to the hungry. (27:7)

If I hadn't been as parched as a salamander in the Sahara, eating dirty grapes off a trail would have sounded ridiculous. It would have been as unthinkable in that canyon as it is to me right now. But because I was desperate to quench my thirst, I was willing to compromise my standards of cuisine and justified eating those grapes.

That's the danger of not finding our everything in God. When we leave those God-shaped holes in our hearts gaping open, we become desperate to fill them. When we're hungry (for God), relationships that would have been an easy "no way" if we were full become irrationally appealing. This often explains why smart, beautiful girls get into relationships with bad boys or why girls committed to their purity compromise their values with guys who don't respect them. Here's a paraphrase of Proverbs 27:7:

> A girl who lets God "make" her is free to say no to
> even a great guy, but a girl who is desperate for love

and attention will be tempted by even destructive relationships.

My prayer for you is that you will be so satisfied in God that you won't be tempted to settle for anything less than the best: a healthy relationship with a godly man, in God's perfect timing. Anything less than that is like eating dirty grapes.

We're going to spend quite a bit of time in the coming chapters dreaming together about what a godly relationship can look like. But we have to let this truth sink down deep into our hearts first: God is enough. You don't need a guy to "make you"—to make you whole, beautiful, desired, precious, confident, joyful, complete, or worthy. And because God is enough—because He is *everything* you need—you're free to hope and dream about the future without making a guy or a relationship into an idol.

Yahweh Rophe, You are the God who heals. I admit that I've been looking to fill the hole in my heart in all the wrong places. I've exchanged the truth of You for lies. Forgive me, Lord. Heal me. Become my everything. I want to be so full of You that I won't crave human love the way I have in the past. I want to worship You, the Maker, not the things You've made. I love You so much, God. Amen.

Discussion Questions

1. *Based on the definition of an idol on page 21, what idols have you unconsciously bowed before?*

2. When we make guys into idols, what are we hoping they'll do for us that only the true God can do?

3. Which of the four lies we explored in this chapter do you struggle with most? Why do you think that is?

4. What do you think about the "hard truth" that God hasn't promised you'll get married? Are you okay with that? Would you be willing to trust God to say no to marriage if it were for His glory and your good?

5. Have you tried to numb the pain of singleness in any unhealthy ways?

6. Take a few minutes to write a letter to God in your journal, giving your heart fully and completely to Him and asking Him to fill it to the brim.

CHAPTER 3

He Can't Make You You

Who do you think you are?

Don't worry, you're not in trouble. I really want to know. When you think about *you*, what comes to mind? Who are you?

When I was a sophomore in high school, I had an awesome English teacher. Mrs. Cornford got us excited about writing and grammar not only because she was young and cool (and not even because half the boys had crushes on her) but also because she got us thinking and writing about things we cared about. Have you ever had a teacher like that? Someone who made school and learning fun? Anyway, our big assignment for the year was to write a series of stories all revolving around one main character. Our character could be anyone we wanted to create. Throughout the year, we wrote stories in the first person (as if we were that character) based on a simple title like, "A Time When I Felt Scared" or "My Best Birthday Ever."

That's when Dakota was born. "Cody" (as I called her for

short) was a Jeep-driving, adventure-loving twenty-year-old with a knack for putting people at ease and a love for everything outdoors. She had strong convictions and loved God. She traveled and studied and felt like the world was at her fingertips. And as much as I denied it when my friends teased me in class, it was pretty obvious that Dakota was my alter ego. She was the me I wanted to be. Sure, it was over-the-top cheeseball literature (I can barely read it now without blushing at my superfluous use of flowery adjectives), but it represented one girl's expression of all the best she saw in herself and who she someday wanted to be. I wanted to be adventurous and kind and strong and confident. And, doggone it, I *still* want a beat-up old Jeep to drive!

When I think about it now, that high school assignment was kind of like a modern-day social media page. Today it's easier than ever just to portray the *you* you want to be and hide all the other stuff. You can post pictures of only your "good side" on your best-hair days, share all the highlights of your life as if they're no big deal, and make it seem like a party follows you everywhere you go. And it'll work: You'll make everyone jealous of your life. But is that the *real* you?

The truth is, as much as I *wanted* to always be adventurous, strong, and perfect like Dakota, I'm just . . . not. And all my imperfections (about which my family could easily bring you up to speed!) are a part of who I am too. Some of them I'm working to change, like being controlling and easily offended. Others will probably just always be part of who I am, like my crooked pinky toe or the way I turn into a cranky mess after 10 p.m.

So when I ask you, "Who do you think you are?" I want

to know more than the Facebook version of you. I want to know who you are when no one is watching (or "following" or "liking") you. I want you to think about all your experiences, shortcomings, strengths, and quirky habits that make up the unique daughter God designed.

Now, let me ask you again: "Who are you?"

Once you've allowed God to fill your deepest longings, like we talked about in the previous chapter, there's still so much about you that's uniquely you. One of the most exciting things about this time of your life is the chance to discover all those things about you that combine to make you the person you are. You get to decide what you'll stand for, what direction you'll take with your life, and what kind of person you want to be. While those decisions might feel stressful sometimes, I can't think of anything more exciting than having the freedom and hope of an open horizon stretching out in front of you!

At this point, you might be wondering who passed me the happy juice. Trust me, I know it's not always easy to believe what God says about you, especially when people all around you seem to be screaming, "You're nothing special!" I say this with all the love in my heart: They're idiots. Don't listen to them. Don't listen to the media, bullies, ungodly friends, or even parents who put you down. God is bigger and He's stronger, and what He says is truer than all the lies Satan can throw at you. But you've got to trust. You've got to believe God and His words. Just like we uncovered those four lies in chapter 2, you're going to have to uncover and chuck out any lies you believe about your worth and identity before you can become the *you* God wants you to be.

Chameleon's Law

You have the power, ability, and *responsibility* to choose who you'll be, and it's important that you make those decisions about yourself before you're in a serious relationship. If you don't, Chameleon's Law will take over. (Lucky for us, this law is way easier to understand than the third law of thermodynamics because I just made it up.)

Chameleon's Law states,

> A girl not grounded in her own identity will adapt to become like the people around her.

Chameleon's Law especially applies to guys and relationships. If a girl isn't confident in her identity, she'll adapt to become like the guy she admires. Just like some chameleon species change color to blend into their surroundings, she changes into whatever she thinks is most desirable. (There's that "desire to be desired" again.)

Let's be honest—it's downright hilarious to watch the ways some girls adapt to become the kind of girl they think their crush would like. He snowboards? She's out buying a board and ski pants. He's the drummer in a band? She becomes a groupie. He's a metro guy? She's ditching her sweats and flip-flops for more sophisticated clothes. He's into camping? She finds herself sleeping on the ground in the middle of nowhere while coyotes pee on her shoes (true story).

Yes, my friend, *I* am "exhibit A" for Chameleon's Law. And while some of the things I discovered through the guys I dated were awesome and have become part of who I am today—like rock climbing and good poetry—other "interests" were destructive. The dark side of Chameleon's Law caused this otherwise-good-girl to drink when my current crush was a partier, ditch class when he was more interested in surfing than studying, and listen to raunchy music because I knew that's what was playing in his Discman (for all you young guns, that's like a prehistoric iPod). Thankfully, those relationships didn't last long, but they did do damage that could have been avoided if I had known who I was before looking for love.

It's so much better to spend your time and energy figuring out what you like and who you are and then waiting for a guy who will complement you. So instead of talking your ear off for pages and pages about the ways God has made you unique, I'd love for *you* to do the talking. Take some time to think about your interests, character, talents, weaknesses, and dreams. I want you to get a little glimpse of what God already knows about you: You are an incredibly unique, perfectly designed daughter of the King. He delights in *you*—who you already are, not what you can pretend to be. And any guy worthy of your heart will feel exactly the same.

This quiz is designed to get you thinking about who you really are. There are no right or wrong answers. You can be as straightforward or as flowery as you feel led, and you can interpret each question however you'd like. I ask only that you be completely honest, as if no one in the world will ever read this. In other words, be you! This is for you and for God.

I've given you space to record your answers here, but if you plan to lend this book to a friend, feel free to write your answers in your journal instead.

Oh, and have fun!

THE "ME" QUIZ

My full name is: _____

I am from: _____

My family is: _____
_____
_____

I'd describe my relationship with my parents as:_____
_____
_____
_____

Three things you might not know about me:

1. _____

2. _____

3. _____

I'm happiest when I: _____
_____
_____

When I'm sad, I usually: _____
_____
_____

Someday I want to: _____
_____
_____
_____

If it weren't for God, I'd probably be: _____
_____
_____

I'm most thankful for God's: _____
_____
_____

My favorite Bible verse is _____ *because:* _____
_____
_____

I'd be devastated if: _____
_____
_____

My friends would describe me as: _____
_____
_____

My favorite things in all the world are: _____
_____
_____

School? I think it's: _____
_____
_____

School would be better if: _____

_____

_____

My biggest regrets are: _____

_____

_____

When I'm twenty-five, I hope I'll be: _____

_____

_____

When I'm fifty, I hope I'll be: _____

_____

_____

I'm drawn to people who: _____

_____

_____

If I could make a living someday doing anything I wanted, I'd:

_____

_____

My three biggest fears are:

　1. _____

　2. _____

　3. _____

I love to read: _____

_____

_____

If I could live anywhere, you'd find me in: _____

_____

_____

_____

Five words that describe my personality are:

1. _____

2. _____

3. _____

4. _____

5. _____

If there were no boys around, I would: _____

_____

_____

My favorite:

MOVIE _____

COLOR _____

PLACE _____

DAY _____

FOOD _____

SEASON _____

GAME OR SPORT _____

I'd describe my style as: _____

_____

_____

Someday I'd like to: _____
_____
_____
_____

Money is like: _____
_____
_____

If I had to give up electronics for a week, I'd: _____
_____
_____
_____

My life would be better if: _____
_____
_____
_____

When I look in the mirror, I see: _____
_____
_____
_____

The five things I love most about myself are:

1. _____

2. _____

3. _____

4. _____

5. _____

If I could change three things about me, I would change:

1. _____

2. _____

3. _____

When no one is looking, I: _____

_____

_____

The most painful thing that has happened to me was: _____

_____

_____

_____

When I'm hurting, I cope by: _____

_____

_____

I feel most loved when someone: _____

_____

_____

Three things I love to do are:

1. _____

2. _____

3. _____

I think this quiz has been: _____

_____

_____

_____

How was that? Not too torturous, I hope! The point of the quiz was simply to get you thinking about just how unique you are. No one else would answer those questions exactly like you did! Maybe you even discovered something new about yourself in the process. I have a feeling you're going to have a good time rereading that little quiz many years from now.

Putting On the New

While we're talking about identity, I should make a distinction. There are people who would tell you you're who you are and you can't do anything about it. That would be fine if sin had never entered the world! But because it did, our hearts are "the most deceitful of all things" and "desperately wicked" (Jeremiah 17:9). None of us knows just how tangled up in sin we really are. That's why we can't always trust ourselves. You can't "be true to you" (like the world tells you to be) because without Christ, the only "true" you is a wicked wretch. Thankfully, God made a way to save us from our sin and doesn't leave us wallowing in our guilt, and He doesn't let His children stay stuck in old sin patterns either.

God calls us to change anything about ourselves that doesn't glorify Him, and He lays out certain qualities that He wants all of His kids to have, regardless of personality. Throughout the Bible, we find commands to take off the old, sinful nature of our lives and put on the new nature—the nature of God. Colossians 3:9-10 says,

> You have stripped off your old sinful nature and all its
> wicked deeds. Put on your new nature, and be renewed

as you learn to know your Creator and become like him.

Think of it this way: If God had made *you* (instead of Eve) for Adam and you had never touched that fruit in the Garden of Eden, what would you be like? Would you be shy? Funny? Adventurous? Artistic? Strong? Laid-back? Those parts of your personality make you *you*. God gave you those characteristics on purpose; He delights in them and wants you to develop them. The sinful habits—the "old sinful nature"—not so much. God wants you to strip off such things as resentment, jealousy, eating disorders, dishonesty, addiction, sexual sin, hate, cruelty, rebellion, and anything else that isn't like Him. Summed up, God wants you to become holy in everything you do because He is holy (see 1 Peter 1:15-16). That's a lot to ask, and He knows it. That's why He hasn't left you to battle sin on your own.

When Jesus rose from the dead, right before He left this earth to be reunited with His Father in heaven, He promised His disciples something: a gift. He told them to stick around in Jerusalem until it came. So there they were, forty days later, praying and worshipping in a secret room. Then *He* came. The Holy Spirit's entrance was nothing if not showy: the sound of wind, the appearance of fire, everyone talking in languages they didn't know. There was no doubt that this was the Spirit of God, ready to get down to business!

Now, get this: That same Holy Spirit lives in you if you are God's child (see 1 Corinthians 6:19). I could go on and on about how blow-your-mind amazing that is, but I'll have to save it for another time. For now, though, one of His many jobs in your life is to mold you into the image of God. In other words, He helps you to become holy—to become more like the God who created you (as Colossians 3:9-10 instructs us). When the Holy Spirit has free reign in your life, He:

- Frees you from the power of sin (see Romans 8:2)
- Produces fruit (character traits) such as love, joy, peace, patience, kindness, goodness, faithfulness, gentleness, and self-control (see Galatians 5:22-23)
- Gives you new thoughts and attitudes (see Ephesians 4:23)
- Helps you to be marked by love, power, and self-discipline (see 2 Timothy 1:7)

God expects His daughters to move past the sinful parts of who we are. Because He loves us, God doesn't want us to stay content living all tangled up in sin. But when the Holy Spirit is at work making us more like Jesus, the rest of our identity—the part God gave us—can be as unique as a fingerprint is to a hand.

Here's an example. God wants me to love others. As His follower, that's a nonnegotiable; it's the way the world will know that I belong to Him (see John 13:35). But how I show love might be very different from the way you show love. I'm just going to tell you now that if we ever get to meet in person, I'm probably going to violate all your personal space and give you a huge hug. I'm working on not making others feel awkward by my where-have-you-been-all-my-life embraces, but it's just in my nature. I'm a hugger, I admit it. Maybe you show your love by telling someone how great she is or by picking her wildflowers when she's had a terrible day. As long as you obey the command to love, you're free to let your obedience take the shape of your unique personality.

Here's another example. Let's say I'm really into sports and I'm a pretty decent volleyball player. My athleticism would be part of who I am. But in my journey toward holiness (through the Holy Spirit's power in my life), I can learn to stop trusting in my athletic skills or boasting about them. I can let God's Word transform me:

> Don't let the wise boast in their wisdom, or the powerful boast in their power, or the rich boast in their riches. But those who wish to boast should boast in this alone: that they truly know me and understand that I am the LORD who demonstrates unfailing love and who brings justice and righteousness to the earth, and that I delight in these things. (JEREMIAH 9:23-24)

If I'm taking God's commands to heart, eventually I'm going to love justice and righteousness more than training for my sport. I might (and probably will) always love to play volleyball, but I'll care even more about truly knowing and understanding the God who gave me a love for the game in the first place. Once again, God and my personality collide to make me a unique, holy mix for His glory and my good.

Are You Interesting?

Only God can make you *you*. He made you unique when He designed you in eternity past, and He continues to make you more beautiful each day through the power of His Spirit in your life. No guy can even come close to that.

Someone (who probably knew my chameleon-ish tendencies) once asked me a question that has always stuck with me: "Are you trying to be interest*ed* or to be interest*ing*?" When we allow our latest crush to define our identity, we focus on being interested in *him*. We become what we think he'll like so he'll be interested in us back. Unfortunately, that rarely (probably more like never) ends well. When we focus instead on just being an interesting person in general—someone who is fun and has hobbies and is confident in who she is—then we become interesting to others, including that guy who might be a good match for us someday. Make sense?

No guy can make you *you*. And I hope this chapter has helped you see why you wouldn't want him to even if he could! You are already on your way to becoming a divine mix of perfectly proportioned interests, godly characteristics, and a flair that is uniquely you. My prayers are with you as you dream and discover and become all that God intended when He so perfectly designed you.

> *My amazing Designer, forgive me for not always*
> *appreciating the specific ways You've made me me. I see*
> *now that no part of who I am was by accident. I want my*
> *whole life—my interests, choices, plans, and desires—to*
> *reflect who You are. I want to make You proud, Daddy.*
> *Help me to fight the temptation to become what I think*
> *the people around me will want. I truly want to be more*
> *like You every single day of my life. Amen.*

Discussion Questions

1. What lies about your identity does Satan hound you with? What does God say about you that contradicts each of those lies?

2. Can you see a pattern of "Chameleon's Law" in your life? Who have you been known to adapt to for acceptance?

3. Do you see any sinful characteristics in your life that need changing? Write them down in your journal with a quick prayer, asking God to help change you through His Spirit.

4. Do you focus more on being interested or interesting?

CHAPTER 4

He Can't Break You

Cassy[5] was sure her left hand would be sporting some bling in just a few months, and the thought made her smile from ear to ear. She had been dating J.R. for nearly five years, and they were finally getting ready to finish their sophomore year in college, the point at which his parents had promised they would finally allow them to get married. In high school they were voted cutest couple, and everyone expected them to live happily ever after. Cassy and J.R. were the poster couple for perfect love. Their friends said things like, "If you two ever break up, there's no hope for the rest of us ever finding a lasting relationship" and "I guess it's possible to find a high school sweetheart after all."

Their friends weren't the only ones sure that a wedding was inevitable. Cassy had known that J.R. was "the one" since she was fifteen. That's why she had given her heart so completely to him and held on so tightly to their relationship. She was sure God would help them make it through anything together— even going to separate colleges—just like they had made it through the ups and downs of dating in high school. They had made it so far already that Cassy couldn't imagine anything getting in the way of their future together now.

Then the bomb hit. On her way home from spending a weekend in their hometown together, she got a text from J.R. saying he couldn't do it anymore and they should just be friends. After five years of giving her heart, body, and soul to him, he broke up with her in a text. *A text!*

Once Cassy gave up begging him to give "them" another try and finally accepted it really was over, her world grew dark. She felt like J.R. had died—the mourning was that intense. It was as if her world had been hit head-on by a semi and she was trapped inside the darkness. She tried to pray, tried to read her Bible, tried to cope, but the pain was so intense that she couldn't go long without tears. She skipped class and avoided her friends. She had to force herself to eat, and even then she battled nausea. Cassy angrily wrestled with questions like, *How could he leave me when I had given him all of me?* and *Why would God let this happen if He loves me?* She genuinely wondered if she would ever be able to live a normal life again.

Cassy isn't alone. One of the top reasons girls come to the Life, Love and God website is to find solace after a heart-wrenching breakup. Here are some of their real and raw admissions:

"I just can't seem to get my life back together."

"I want to give up on life."

"I feel really empty, worthless, and depressed."

"Knowing that he has forgotten about me and moved on makes me so sad, and it's making me go crazy!"

"I started to drink, hoping the pain will go away."

"My heart feels like it's ripping apart because of him."

"It feels like a mini end-of-the-world."

Have you ever felt like that? Have you ever been broken by a breakup? Have you ever been broken by rejection, even though no "relationship" ever took place?

This chapter is a hard one for me to write because if you've been hurt, I'd rather be sitting with you on my couch, tissue box planted squarely between us, reaching over for a hug every so often (I believe I've already confessed to you my weakness for overabundant embraces). I pray that what I'm going to say in these pages won't come across as insensitive or uncaring but that you'll be able to hear the pain in my voice as I urge you to see there's a better way. Guys don't have to break you.

Did you catch that? You don't ever have to be broken by a guy—not ultimately. Pain, yes; utter destruction, no. Let me clarify. Anytime you open up to someone—whether boy, girl, young or old, boyfriend or grandma—you're opening up to the possibility of both joy and pain. Relationships are messy things, as you know. I'm not saying you should avoid opening up to a guy just so you won't feel pain. Pain and a little heartache are both part of life. The joy that comes from healthy relationships makes the pain worth it, right?

What I *am* talking about is avoiding the life-shattering variety of heartbreak—a pain so deep you can't see past it. I'm talking about the pain of divorce. *Divorce?* Yes, divorce—and yes, even before you're technically married.

If you allow a guy to make you—when you find your worth, identity, happiness, and contentment in him—then it will feel like divorce when the relationship ends.

I'm sure someone is going to label me extreme on this, but the stakes are too high not to talk about it. When you *act* like you're married—emotionally, spiritually, and physically—the only difference between a breakup and a divorce is that you don't need a lawyer for the former! As Cassy learned, it hurts just the same, it damages your heart just the same, and it has long-term consequences just the same. She's not alone. The way most people date today mimics marriage. The way *I* often dated mimicked marriage, and I have the scars to prove it. The good news is that you don't have to go through the date-divorce-date-divorce cycle that has devastated so many hearts. Even if you've been there before, you can stop letting guys break you today and for all your tomorrows.

A Heart Built on Rock

Here's the simple secret to sparing your heart from emotional divorce: A guy can't break you if God is your strength. Let's really think this through. We've already looked at what it means to let God "make" you, but what does it mean to have God as your strength?

Jesus once told a story about what it means to have a life built on the "rock" of God—to find strength in the solid mass of everything God is and has promised us. If He were going to tell the same story to a group of us girls right here in the twenty-first century, I image that *maybe* He would tell it something like this:

> Those who listen to My teaching and actually follow it
> are wise. They're like a girl who finds her strength in God.
> Though her boyfriend of five years breaks his promises,

though he cheats on her or breaks up with her in a text, she won't be devastated because her heart is built on the bedrock of God's truth. But the girl who hears God's instructions to find her everything in Him yet turns to guys for her worth instead is foolish, like a girl who builds her heart on sand. When that girl's boyfriend breaks his promises, cheats on her, or breaks up with her in a text, her whole world will collapse with a mighty crash.[6]

That's what I mean when I say guys don't have to break you. If you choose to enter into a relationship with any guy—this month or twenty years from now—you *will* feel pain, either through the normal ups and downs of love or when that relationship eventually ends. But God wants to be your rock! He wants you to build your life on Him so He can be the firm foundation that allows you to weather life's storms. How do you build your life on Him? Jesus gave us the answer in Matthew 7:24: by listening to and actually following His teaching. We've already looked at some of that teaching as it relates to love and relationships, such as:

- Let God change your thought life (see Romans 12:2). to thoughts that are true, honorable, and right (see Philippians 4:8).
- Keep God first in your life. No idols—not even really hot ones! (see Exodus 20:3,5).
- Learn to know your Creator and become like Him (see Colossians 3:10).

In the chapters to come, we're going to discover more of God's truth as it relates to guys, relationships, and our hearts. As you come across those dating commands, jot them down on a journal page titled "God's Instructions for Relationships." Then *follow* them! If you do, you won't ultimately be broken by a breakup like a girl who builds her heart on the sand. There *is* a way to find your match made in heaven without risking feeling really empty, worthless, and depressed by a breakup. Heartache, sure. But you should never allow a relationship with *any* guy get you to the point that you want to give up on life if he leaves you. A life built on God is stronger than that!

What to Do with the Pain

Let's go back to the pain for a minute; I definitely don't want to gloss over it. Even when we've been guarding our hearts and honoring God in our relationships, if dreams are broken, it hurts! I'm well acquainted with Proverbs 13:12: "Hope deferred makes the heart sick." And, unfortunately, I had more than one emotional divorce before I learned to build my heart on my strong God.

If you've been devastated by a broken relationship or if you know someone who has, I hope this section will help you weather the storm gracefully. And if you're single today, just tuck this away in your mind for a rough day in the (hopefully very distant) future.

So you met a great guy and you *really* liked him and then he liked you back and you thought life couldn't get any better. But then he changed his mind (or you did), and now your heart feels like it went through the spin cycle in the washing machine and you're not sure what to think or how to feel or what to do. Well, you have a few options. One, you could sink into an emotional black hole of tears and despair. Two, you could try to drink alcohol or eat ice cream or run excessively or harm yourself to try to numb the pain. Three, you could ignore your pain by stuffing it all inside and pretending everything is just peachy. Or, four, you could go a much more effective (and altogether healthier) route: Turn to God.

Chances are you've probably been told before to turn to God with your pain. Maybe you've even tried it. But if you're like most girls, you might be wondering what in the world that actually means. How does one turn to God when He isn't (last I checked) taking appointments for grief counseling? How can you find your strength in God when your heart feels like melting Jell-O and you'd rather run away from everything than face it? First you have to cling to God. Then you have to mourn your loss. Lastly, remember hope. Let's take a closer look at those three steps together.

Cling to God.

My six-year-old daughter, Ryan, loves the aquarium. She'd go every day if she could. But there's a shark tank there that scares the tar out of her. I don't know who thought it would be a good idea to play the *Jaws* theme song over the speakers in a dimly lit shark exhibit meant for kids, but there you have it. And every time we visit the aquarium, she starts getting nervous three exhibits back, right about the coral reef zone. She doesn't ask me to hold her hand. Oh no. She won't go past that shark tank unless she's in a full body wrap: arms squeezing my neck, legs like a corset around my waist, head buried in my hair. She clings to me for dear life.

That's what I mean when I say you'll have to cling to God through your heartache. I'm not talking about the occasional prayer asking Him to help you through a tight spot. This is more than lip service; you're going to have to hold on tight, like a full body wrap around your Daddy. Read, pray, journal. Repeat. Repeat again. Keep repeating until you can put one foot in front of the other and walk—even if wobbly kneed—forward.

If you're not in the habit of spending time with God, this is going to take extra self-control. You're going to need more than a five-minute devotional each morning. When you have to cling to God, you've got to read your Bible as though your life depended on it. You've got to pray with a sense of determination, dependence, and earnestness. Yes, that means time—lots of time—with God, which means some other things might need to be put on hold. So turn off your computer and your phone; say *adios* to social media for a bit. Yeah, I know that sounds crazy, but desperate times call for desperate measures. This is for your survival! God is enough for you in your hour of need, but you have to cling to Him instead of to your friends, your distractions, and your own self-pity.

Even if you're not into journaling, may I suggest that this would be a great time to make an exception? Two reasons why: One, even though it takes work, journaling is a really good way to sort through your feelings and get down to the truth. King David's psalms were like that. Many of them are like journal entries that progress from venting his feelings to stating truths about who God is and why He can be trusted. Then David's feelings would come around again to acceptance, peace, and hope. The second reason to keep a journal through the dark times in life is as a memorial to what God does in your heart. I can't tell you how cool it is to read through old journals and praise God for answering prayer after prayer I so desperately prayed during the storms I faced. God is so faithful! And it's good for His children to remember His goodness years down the road. Remembering what He *has* done gives us faith to trust in what He *will* do. And thus ends my little infomercial for journaling. Now let's go back to the Bible reading for a minute.

If you're not sure where to start reading, here are some verses I found comforting when my own heart was breaking and I was desperate for God. But by all means, don't stop here. These are just to whet your appetite:

You keep track of all my sorrows.
> You have collected all my tears in your bottle.
> You have recorded each one in your book. (PSALM 56:8)

Give all your worries and cares to God, for he cares about you. (1 PETER 5:7)

God has not given us a spirit of fear and timidity, but of power, love, and self-discipline. (2 TIMOTHY 1:7)

Seek the Kingdom of God above all else, and live righteously, and he will give you everything you need. (MATTHEW 6:33)

When doubts filled my mind,
> your comfort gave me renewed hope and cheer.
> > (PSALM 94:19)

Jesus said, "Come to me, all of you who are weary and carry heavy burdens, and I will give you rest. Take my yoke upon you. Let me teach you, because I am humble and gentle at heart, and you will find rest for your souls. For my yoke is easy to bear, and the burden I give you is light." (MATTHEW 11:28-30)

Wherever your treasure is, there the desires of your heart will also be. (MATTHEW 6:21)

If God cares so wonderfully for wildflowers that are here today and thrown into the fire tomorrow, he will certainly care for you. Why do you have so little faith? (MATTHEW 6:30)

Always be full of joy in the Lord. I say it again—rejoice! Let everyone see that you are considerate in all you do. Remember, the Lord is coming soon.

Don't worry about anything; instead, pray about everything. Tell God what you need, and thank him for all he has done. Then you will experience God's peace, which exceeds anything we can understand. His peace will guard your hearts and minds as you live in Christ Jesus.

And now, dear brothers and sisters, one final thing. Fix your thoughts on what is true, and honorable, and right, and pure, and lovely, and admirable. Think about things that are excellent and worthy of praise. (PHILIPPIANS 4:4-8)

You go before me and follow me.
    You place your hand of blessing on my head.
Such knowledge is too wonderful for me,
    too great for me to understand!

I can never escape from your Spirit!
    I can never get away from your presence!
If I go up to heaven, you are there;
    if I go down to the grave, you are there.

If I ride the wings of the morning,
  if I dwell by the farthest oceans,
even there your hand will guide me,
  and your strength will support me. . . .

How precious are your thoughts about me, O God.
  They cannot be numbered!
I can't even count them;
  they outnumber the grains of sand!
And when I wake up,
  you are still with me! (PSALM 139:5-10,17-18)

I will praise the LORD at all times.
  I will constantly speak his praises.
I will boast only in the LORD;
  let all who are helpless take heart.
Come, let us tell of the LORD's greatness;
  let us exalt his name together.

I prayed to the LORD, and he answered me.
  He freed me from all my fears.
Those who look to him for help will be radiant with joy;
  no shadow of shame will darken their faces.
In my desperation I prayed, and the LORD listened;
  he saved me from all my troubles.
For the angel of the LORD is a guard;
  he surrounds and defends all who fear him.

Taste and see that the LORD is good.
  Oh, the joys of those who take refuge in him!
Fear the LORD, you his godly people,
  for those who fear him will have all they need.

Even strong young lions sometimes go hungry,
> but those who trust in the Lord will lack no good
> > thing. . . .

The Lord hears his people when they call to him for help.
> He rescues them from all their troubles.
The Lord is close to the brokenhearted;
> he rescues those whose spirits are crushed.
The righteous person faces many troubles,
> but the Lord comes to the rescue each time.
> > (PSALM 34:1-10,17-19)

Mourn the loss.

The next step in turning to God is to really allow yourself to mourn the loss of your relationship. It's important to wait on this step until you're clinging to God because if you try to mourn while your heart is built on sand, you're going to be a certifiable emotional wreck.

When your heart is hurting, sometimes you just have to *allow* it to hurt. You don't have to be afraid of pain. You don't have to be ashamed of tears. A good friend once described pain like a wave. Have you ever watched someone try to get out past the breaking waves into the deeper ocean? The best way to get past a wave isn't to swim over the top. If you try to do that, you end up getting slapped in the face by the top of the breaker and get a mouth full of saltwater. The best way to get past a wave is to take a deep breath and dive right into the center of it. You feel the surge of the water flowing past you, and then you surface safely on the other side. Pain is like that. If you try to fight against it, determined not to feel sadness, you're going to end up getting slapped in the face with unresolved emotions and get a mouthful of bitterness and fear. But if you take a deep breath and dive into the wave of pain, after the surge of emotions flows past you, you'll surface safely on the other side.

So go ahead and mourn the loss of your relationship. As long as you're clinging to God, His truth will keep you from ultimate despair and you can let yourself be sad that it's over. You can cry. You can wish things had turned out differently. You can cry a little more. Then you can forgive and move on and remember that there's hope for tomorrow.

Remember hope.

Hope is a powerful thing. In fact, the apostle Paul listed it as one of the three things that will last forever (along with faith and love; see 1 Corinthians 13:13). At the end of the day, once you've clung to God and allowed yourself to mourn the loss of that relationship, hope is what allows you to smile at the future. Hope is knowing that the sun will come out again, you'll find joy, and God will continue to bless and guide you in life. It's knowing that just because this relationship didn't last forever doesn't mean you won't find someone to spend the rest of your life with.

Hope allows you to hold your head high in dignity and know that there is nothing wrong with you—that things didn't fall apart because you weren't good enough, pretty enough, or cool enough. Hope trusts that if marriage is what's best for you, God will bring the right man at just the right time (this one just wasn't *him*). Sure, "hope deferred makes the heart sick," but hope chooses to focus on the second part of Proverbs 13:12: "A dream fulfilled is a tree of life."

Most of all, hope knows that no matter how hard things get

in life, you have all you need in God! He has given you salvation, forgiveness, the Holy Spirit, an inheritance with Christ, and the promise of eternity with Him! What more could we possibly need?

Even though God's daughters will feel pain in this life, there's no excuse for us to mourn the loss of earthly relationships like the people around us who don't have hope (see 1 Thessalonians 4:13). If you belong to God, you have access to the wellspring of life and hope and joy! I pray that you'll be able to keep that healthy perspective even in the midst of a broken heart. And, like Paul, I also "pray that your hearts will be flooded with light so that you can understand the confident *hope* he has given to those he called—his holy people who are his rich and glorious inheritance" (Ephesians 1:18, emphasis added).

If He Hasn't Made You

> Call on me when you are in trouble,
>   and I will rescue you,
>   and you will give me glory. (Psalm 50:15)

If you get only one thing out of this book, I hope it is this: God is enough. And if you can learn that, believe it, and live it—if you'll allow God to make you who you are and base your worth on who He is—then no guy will ever be able to break you. Let's say it together: "If he hasn't made me, he can't break me." God is enough! You don't need to turn to a guy to find your identity, purpose, or worth.

Do you believe that? Really and truly, do you believe that?

If you don't, you're going to be rocked by emotional divorce if your boyfriend, fiancé, or even husband leaves you. But if you do believe it—if you've accepted that God is enough and built your heart on the Rock—then you're ready to move on to the next step with me: finding your guy without getting crushed.

There *is* a way to find your guy without going through the heart-wrenching pain of emotional divorce. The key? Don't act like you're married until you are. You owe it to yourself to protect your heart from needless pain by considering a different way to find your match. Judging by the number of heartbroken girls out there, the "normal" way of dating sure doesn't seem to be working! So as we jump into the second half of this book, will you consider a better way with me?

> *Father, I know that You are enough for me. Help me live like I believe that! When my heart is breaking, I want to turn to You. Please keep Your promise to be close to me when I'm brokenhearted. When my world feels dark, shine Your light brightly all around me. I trust You; I need You; I find my hope in You. It's because of You that I can smile at the future even when I don't understand today. Amen.*

Discussion Questions

1. *Have you ever been "broken" by a guy? How did you cope with the pain? Was it healthy?*

2. *Do you think it's true that a breakup can feel like a divorce? Have you or someone you know experienced pain like that when a relationship ended?*

3. *What are three practical ways that you can turn to God in the middle of heartache?*

4. *Which Bible verses have spoken to your heart when you were in deep pain?*

5. *If dating like you're married leads to emotional divorce when you break up, how can you protect your heart from needless pain?*

Part 2

FINDING YOUR GUY WITHOUT GETTING CRUSHED

CHAPTER 5

Is There a Better Way?
(To Date or Not to Date?)

If we were building a house, we could say we've just laid the foundation—one broad, solid, unshakable foundation. Understanding that only God can make you whole, only God can make you *you*, and no guy can ultimately either make or break you is the bedrock of everything we're going to talk about from here till the very last page. Now that you understand how God is the only one who can truly make you happy, make you feel worthy and beautiful, end your loneliness, and be the one constant in your life; now that you've marveled at who God has made you to be and that no guy deserves the honor of robbing your identity; and now that you have confidence that no earthly relationship can ultimately break you as long as your heart is built on God's Word and His strength—*now* we can talk about what a godly relationship can look like. (How's that for a really long sentence?)

This part really excites me because I do believe there is a much better way to find your match than what most people are trying, and I love to help my sisters find the sweet spot of God's will for their lives. God designed love and romance and marriage, and I am 100 percent sure that if marriage is God's best for your life, He will bring just the right man at just the right time as you keep your eyes focused where they belong: on Him! It's fun to dream and hope and wonder and prepare your heart for that day, and I want to join you on this exciting journey.

If you're wondering whether I'm going to tell you that dating is okay, to kiss it good-bye, to give it a chance, or to pack up and move to a monastery in some remote village of Spain, let me put your mind at ease right now. (Or if you were *hoping* I would give you a cut-and-dried method, then I am sorry to disappoint.) There are a few specific methods out there that describe what relationships should look like before you tie the marriage knot (and some of them are really good), but that's not the point of this book. My goal is to give you God's Word and then let you decide the best possible way for you to follow it wholeheartedly.

I believe that the Bible is God's road map for our lives and that it "is useful to teach us what is true and to make us realize what is wrong in our lives. . . . God uses it to prepare and equip his people to do every good work" (2 Timothy 3:16-17). In other words, I believe that God's Word has the answers to our questions and is relevant to every issue we face, including how to find our guys. According to 2 Timothy 3:16-17, the Bible is useful for teaching us God's truth about guy-girl relationships and helping us see where we've been getting it wrong. God uses His Word to prepare you to find your mate the right way (a *very* good work!).

So here's the burning question: What does the Bible say about dating?

Nothing. Nada. Zilch. The Bible doesn't mention dating one time. Why? Because it didn't exist back when the Bible was written. From the life of Abraham to the time of Christ, you were either single or you were married (with a brief engagement period in between). Dating (or going out, or being a couple, or—for the retro-lovers out there—going steady) is a relatively new phenomenon. Virtually no one dated a hundred years ago, and it's still crazy talk for much of the world. Even though the Bible doesn't mention dating, it *does* give us plenty of guidelines to evaluate whether we should be dating (or courting, or staying single, or arranging marriages, or whatever!) and how to go about finding our guys in a godly way. You might be surprised just how many verses give us truths about God's design for pairing up.

You're going to want to have the journal page you titled "God's Instructions for Relationships" (see chapter 4) handy as we dive in.

Instruction #1: Treat each other like family.

The apostle Paul loved this guy named Timothy like a son. He wrote him quite a few letters (two of which are preserved in our Bibles) that encouraged and taught him the ins and outs of life with God and ministry in the church he led. Because Timothy wasn't married and was probably quite the eligible bachelor, Paul wanted to make sure he understood how to interact with everyone in his spiritual care, especially the young ladies. Paul told Timothy that just as he should treat the older men and women as he would treat his own mother and father, he should also treat the younger men and women as he would his own brothers and sisters. Here are Paul's words:

> Never speak harshly to an older man, but appeal to him
> respectfully as you would to your own father. Talk to
> younger men *as you would to your own brothers.* Treat
> older women as you would your mother, and treat
> younger women *with all purity as you would your own
> sisters.* (1 TIMOTHY 5:1-2, EMPHASIS ADDED)

In the body of Christ, we're family. That means until you're married, you should treat all your brothers in Christ as just that: brothers. And those brothers-from-other-mothers should treat you like . . . wait for it . . . sisters. Notice that Paul emphasizes that the brother-sister relationship should be "with all purity." Makes sense, doesn't it? Who would want to kiss her own brother? Eeew! Gives me the creeps just thinking about it! But that's exactly what God says we're doing when we cross physical boundaries with any Christian guy who is not our husband. He's either your brother or your husband (with a brief engagement period in between). Brothers and sisters are not exclusive, they don't text each other incessantly, and they certainly don't stare longingly into each other's eyes. And "siblings with benefits"? They'd get locked up in most states! (If you're done gagging now, let's move on.)

One of the things I love about God is He gives us instructions never to rob us of our joy but always to heighten it! God tells us to treat guys as brothers (and vice versa) because He knows having that mind-set will save us from making a mess of our lives and will bless our socks off. If we wait to act like we're married until we actually are, we won't suffer the emotional and physical consequences of premarital divorce. Instead, we can enjoy all the benefits of family life: having a ton of cool older and younger brothers to look out for us, teach us, and protect us. What girl wouldn't love that?

I think this command, to treat each other like brothers and sisters, is the umbrella over all the other instructions about guy-girl relationships in the Bible. If you can get this one down, the rest will be cake (including this next one)!

Instruction #2: Don't get trapped.

Paul not only taught believers to treat each other like the family we are, he also taught a lot about freedom. His reasoning went something like this: God paid a crazy high price to free us from our sin, so we'd be idiots to get all tangled up in it again (see Galatians 5:1 and virtually any other of Paul's books). He taught that if we truly understand just how dead meat we were in our sin—how far from God and how helpless we were to ever get close to Him on our own—then we'd guard the freedom Christ gave us with dear life. Sin brings death. Jesus gives freedom. And once we've tasted that sweet freedom, we should be doing everything we can to both enjoy it and protect it. If we're serious about protecting that freedom, sometimes we're going to have to say no to things we're technically "allowed" to do. Here's how Paul put it:

> You say, "I am allowed to do anything"—but not everything is good for you. And even though "I am allowed to do anything," I must not become a slave to anything. (1 CORINTHIANS 6:12)

Even though Christ freed us from having to follow all the detailed rules and regulations that Old Covenant Jews had to follow, we still have to be smart about what we allow ourselves to do if we're going to protect our priceless freedom. This verse applies to so many areas of a Christian's life! In the world of love and relationships, we could ask ourselves this: Is this guy good for me? Is this dating model good for me? Would this guy or way of finding my mate make me a slave to anything (to the relationship, to the guy, and so forth)?

In another letter to the Corinthians, Paul accused some of them of being "limited by [their] own affections" (2 Corinthians 6:12, HCSB). That phrase has always stuck with me: limited by their own affections. Paul wasn't specifically talking about relationships in that verse, but still, what a challenge! Do we love the freedom from sin that Jesus has given us enough to avoid anything—any relationship, any way of dating, *anything*—that would limit it? Would you steer clear of (or end) a relationship that caused you to be far from God or to focus on the wrong things or to sin in any way?

Heavy stuff! But I'm afraid, as girls, we're limited by our own affections way too often, and it's time for that to change. It's time that we stop using our liberty as an opportunity to get emotionally and physically tangled up with guys. So whatever dating model you choose, make sure you're not getting yourself trapped—trapped in sin or trapped by your own affections.

Instruction #3: Team up with a believer.

This one is pretty short and sweet because the Bible is crystal clear on the subject: If you follow God, you'd best team up with someone who does the same. Dating or marrying someone who isn't a Christian is just not even an option if you want to be in the sweet spot of God's will.

> Don't team up with those who are unbelievers. How can righteousness be a partner with wickedness? How can light live with darkness? What harmony can there be between Christ and the devil? How can a believer be a partner with an unbeliever? And what union can there be between God's temple and idols? For we are the temple of the living God. As God said: "I will live in them and walk among them. I will be their God, and they will be my people." (2 CORINTHIANS 6:14-16)

Yes, we've all heard the stories of girls (or guys) who fell for someone who wasn't a believer and they dated them anyway and ended up leading them to the Lord and everyone lived happily ever after. And I am thrilled that God gave those individuals grace and blessed them with happy marriages! But God does not promise that, and I've heard many more stories of God-loving girls who chose to date "really nice"—even "spiritual"—unbelievers and ended up with broken hearts or far from God or in very difficult relationships, especially once they got married and had kids and had to decide what they would teach their children about God.

I can tell you firsthand that there is a never-ending stream of blessings when two single believers are both following hard after God and then decide to follow hard after Him together! Until you're married, it's hard to imagine why being on the same spiritual team is so important. But all these little things come up in marriage—from how you'll spend your money to who will work—that are influenced by your views of God. It's hard enough to build a healthy marriage without different spiritual beliefs getting in the way! Do yourself a favor and make sure whoever you team up with will lead you closer to the Lord, not further away.

Instruction #4: Choose a godly guy.

Speaking of leading you closer to the Lord, let's talk a little about what kind of guy God wants you to look for. We're going to spend a whole chapter on this a little later, but let me give you one solid piece of advice here: Whether you date or court or anything in between, wait for a guy who loves God more than he loves you. Why is that so important? Because God has given husbands some serious shoes to fill, and there's no way they can do it on their own.

> For husbands, this means love your wives, just as Christ loved the church. He gave up his life for her to make her holy and clean, washed by the cleansing of God's word. . . . Each man must love his wife as he loves himself. (EPHESIANS 5:25-26,33)

Yeah, think a guy can love you with the never-stopping, selfless, purifying, fervent love Christ has for His bride on his own? No way. He might very well want to, but if your man is not constantly connected to the source of that love—by loving God more than he loves you—he's going to fail miserably.

So ask yourself this while you're thinking about what finding your match might look like: *How would a godly guy pursue me? What views would he have about dating or courting or finding his wife? Would he expect me to act as if I'm married—emotionally or physically—before we actually are? How would he love me with*

Christ's love as we get to know each other and decide whether we're meant to be?

Instruction #5: Honor your parents.

Right after the verse we just looked at comes another important guideline for the world of dating:

> Children, obey your parents because you belong to the Lord, for this is the right thing to do. "Honor your father and mother." This is the first commandment with a promise: If you honor your father and mother, "things will go well for you, and you will have a long life on the earth." (EPHESIANS 6:1-3)

Notice Paul didn't say, "Obey your parents because they're cool and because they always understand you." No, he says to obey them because you belong to the Lord and that makes obeying them the right thing to do. I'm not going to lie—this is a really, really, *really* hard command to follow sometimes. (I think that might be why God made it the first command with a promise that He'll bless us if we listen!) Unless your parents have asked you to do something that directly violates God's laws and will for your life, your job is to obey with a good attitude. (Have I mentioned that this one is *really* hard to follow?)

So what does this mean for your love life? Well, unless your parents ask you to do something opposite of God's will (like hook up with someone who isn't a believer), then you've got to follow their rules about dating as long as they are your authority.[7] Here are some not-so-popular rules parents have been known to enforce:

"You can't date until you're a certain age" (fifteen, eighteen, and so forth).

"No kissing."

"You can go on a date if you're in a group."

"We have to meet him before you can go out with him."

"We don't want you to date, but you can be courted."

"You can date when pigs fly."

Yes, we've all heard the overprotective dad joke: "Sure you can date—when you're thirty!" But in all seriousness, there are lots of reasons God has given you parents, and one reason is to be the gatekeeper of your purity. Unfortunately, not enough parents are taking that all-important job seriously enough. If your parents are some of the few who are serious about protecting you, please don't buck against it. They're just trying to do their job—a job God has given them and for which they'll be held accountable.

So whether your parents' rules make perfect sense or seem ridiculously arbitrary, make sure your decisions about dating (who and when and how) fall in line with their wishes. Even if their rules truly aren't fair or needed, God promises to bless you if you obey Him on this one.

Oh, and if you're not sure what your parents' rules are about dating, now would be a really great time to ask! (Bonus points: Ask them even if you're already "on your own.")

Instruction #6: Be holy.

Another biblical command we can apply to love and dating is to be holy. First Peter 1:13-16 says,

Think clearly and exercise self-control. . . . Live as God's obedient children. Don't slip back into your old ways of living to satisfy your own desires. You didn't know any better then. But now you must be holy in everything you do, just as God who chose you is holy. For the Scriptures say, "You must be holy because I am holy."

To be holy means to be "set apart." You could think of it as having a heart free from anything that doesn't properly belong there. God wants His children to be different from the world around us; He wants our hearts to be wholly His and wholly pure.

So how can we follow this command to "be holy" in our dating life? When it comes to guys and love, what "doesn't properly belong" in our lives? Sexual immorality is a big one, and we're going to spend a whole chapter unpacking what being holy means. But it's more than not having sex; God wants your heart to be pure too. In chapter 2, we talked a lot about not making guys into idols. God has to be *numero uno*! But let's look back at 1 Peter 1:14, "Don't slip back into your old ways of living *to satisfy your own desires*" (emphasis added). Part of being holy means choosing a dating model that is others-focused, not self-focused. If you're dating to scratch an itch, you're dating for the wrong reasons. Our purpose in every romantic relationship should be to serve, give to, and love someone, hopefully for the rest of our lives.

Instruction #7: Don't settle for less than true love.

The point of any form of dating is to find lasting love, right? If your heart longs for a deep and true love, why mess around with anything less? What would be the point of giving *any* part of your heart to a guy who isn't committed to loving you with the real deal—the *real* kind of love? First Corinthians 13 describes true love this way:

> Love is patient and kind. Love is not jealous or boastful or proud or rude. It does not demand its own way. It is not irritable, and it keeps no record of being wronged. It does not rejoice about injustice but rejoices whenever the truth wins out. Love never gives up, never loses faith, is always hopeful, and endures through every circumstance. . . . Three things will last forever—faith, hope, and love—and the greatest of these is love. (1 CORINTHIANS 13:4-7,13)

That's *true* love. Remember how the Bible says that God is love (see 1 John 4:8)? Well, as a society, we've twisted that verse to read, "Love is God." We worship love, guys, marriage, and sex. But real love doesn't pretend to be ultimate; real love bends the knee to God. If you want to find your match without getting crushed, then don't idolize fake love. Instead, wait for the real deal. Real love between a guy and a girl always recognizes that God is number one and worships Him alone.

I'd add that waiting for real love probably means waiting until you're ready and old enough to commit to a 1 Corinthians 13 kind of love yourself. Trying to love a guy "through every circumstance" when you're in high school isn't very realistic. Now, this is Jessie talking here, not God, but I'd say don't start dating or courting or whatever you're planning to do until you're old enough to actually get married. That's the point of dating, right? To find a husband? Window shopping when you really don't have the money to spare always ends with a regrettable purchase. And dating before you're ready or able to commit to marriage always ends with a (usually painful) breakup. Trying to fill a God-shaped void with guys, remember, is only going to leave you empty and addicted to a cheap substitute called human love.

Instruction #8: Consider that "normal" isn't always best

Just because everybody seems to be doing something doesn't mean it's best. In fact, if most of the world—a world that doubts God's existence and rejects His commands—is doing something, there's a good chance it's *not* best! King Solomon warned against swimming with the crowd in many proverbs, like this one:

> There is a path before each person that seems right, but it ends in death. (14:12)

Talk about a reason to go against the norm! I'm sure you're not looking for death (even the allegorical variety) anytime soon. Question everything, including whether the world has got it right when it comes to dating. We have to be willing to ask ourselves those hard questions, like whether the path we're taking *seems* right or *is* right. If you're not sure, another proverb gives us a fail-safe:

> Fear of the LORD is a life-giving fountain; it offers escape from the snares of death. (14:27)

To fear the Lord means, in a nutshell, to honor, respect, and obey Him. So if you're searching the Scriptures and honestly doing your best to honor and respect God by following His commands, you'll escape death and, incidentally, avoid getting crushed. That's good news, isn't it?

As believers, our lives should look mysterious to the rest of the world. They should look different. Do they? Or do God's sons and daughters love, date, and mess around with each other just like the rest of the world? Sobering questions. We're called to walk worthy of the gospel. That means your love life should reflect the redemption God has offered you.

And although we should be thoughtful and intentional about what path we're following, believers should also be carefree about love because we are eternally free! I love this perspective from King Solomon:

> Young people, it's wonderful to be young! Enjoy every minute of it. Do everything you want to do; take it all in. But remember that you must give an account to God for everything you do. (ECCLESIASTES 11:9)

That mind-set goes against the norm too, doesn't it? Most girls are so preoccupied with their relationship status that they miss out on enjoying the best years of their lives! Or maybe they live like they won't have to answer to anyone and live in sin and make a mess of their lives. But as for you? I know you're going to find a healthy balance, just like Solomon taught. I believe you're going to enjoy being young (whether single or in a relationship) and make decisions in light of God and His plan for your life. You're a smart girl! Choose wisely.

The Choice Is Yours

So, is there a better way than the conventional dating philosophy of date-divorce-date-divorce? Absolutely. But what that model looks like in *your* love story depends on you. You have the freedom to choose. As long as you're following God's guide-lines for relationships, you can choose to date or court or stay single or make up your own self-named relationship model. Ask God what His will is for your love life and then listen for the Holy Spirit to guide you into truth. Jesus said that those who listen and obey His commands are like the man who built his house on the rock. You can't go wrong with that.

And be honest with yourself! You should know yourself well enough to know whether you can, say, date one-on-one while still following God's guidelines. A wise girl knows her limita-tions and steers clear of the path of death—for God's glory and her own good!

One final thought as we wrap up this chapter: When we're talk-ing about any of God's rules, there's a danger of starting to judge each other. Let's remember this isn't a matter of salvation, okay? I truly believe that God cares more about the unity of His body than about convincing others to date a certain way. Here's my little paraphrase of Romans 14:1-6, which explains what I mean:

> Accept others' views of dating, and don't argue with them
> about what they think is right or wrong. For instance, one
> girl believes it's okay to date when she's fifteen. Another
> believer is waiting until a man pursues and courts her.
> Those who feel free to date must not look down on
> those who don't. And those who think dating isn't God's
> best plan must not condemn those who do—they're still
> believers, for heaven's sake! Who are we to judge each
> other? Only God gets to decide whether each of us is
> right or wrong. Our job is to focus on our own walk with
> God and be 100 percent sure in our own minds that

we're doing what God wants us to do. If you date, do it to honor the Lord. If you court, do it to honor the Lord. If you choose to stay single, then do it to honor the Lord!

Does that make sense? As much as I want each of God's daughters to be confident and ready to defend her view of dating, I also know that we have to be willing to give each other grace and room to find our own "better way" to date. We are each a work in progress!

Speaking of progress, I pray you've taken some steps forward in figuring out what God wants you to do when it comes to dating and possibly finding your future husband. Revel in the freedom God gives you, honor Him always, and obey His guidelines for relationships—then you'll be well on your way to finding your guy without getting crushed!

Gracious Father, thank You for giving me the Bible, which holds everything I need to know about life and love and relationships and honoring You. Light up the path I'm walking on so I can see whether it's a path toward true love or a path toward emotional death. I want to honor You in everything I do, including the way I date—or don't date. Make good on Your promise to bless me as I follow hard after You. Amen.

Discussion Questions

1. *Before reading this chapter, what were your views about different dating models? Have your views changed at all?*

2. Of the eight "Instructions for Relationships," which do you think would be the hardest to follow? Why?

3. What does it mean to talk to a guy like he's your brother? How should a guy treat you if you are his sister?

4. What rules, if any, have your parents given you about dating?

5. The ultimate choice of how to date is up to you (as long as you can follow God's guidelines within that model). What might be the best way for you personally to find your lifelong love without getting crushed? Why? Write those thoughts down in your journal.

CHAPTER 6

Finding Mr. (Im)Perfect

Prince Charming.

His name evokes early memories of childhood dreams of romance. In the years since Prince Charming's debut as Cinderella's dashing beau in 1950, his name has come to mean everything good, handsome, and suave we dream about in a guy. And who wouldn't fall for the tall, dark, and handsome hero of *Cinderella* fame? Apparently, every eligible girl in the kingdom had eyes on him, lookin' all fine in his gold and red military suit. All the ladies were drooling over those broad shoulders, that perfect helmet of dark hair, and that stark-white, uni-tooth smile. Prince Charming was perfect.

It's easy for a guy to be "perfect" when he's super cute and hardly speaks a word. In the world of Disney romances, there's no reality to mess with the illusion of flawlessness. But what about those of us who live in the real world? How do we find our version of Prince Charming when we don't have little mice to make our clothes or a fairy godmother to hook us up with a sweet ride? How do we know if a guy is "the one" when God doesn't play a romantic soundtrack as our future spouse enters the room for the first time?

I'm sure you've seen the way different girls try to find their guys. Some wait for the proverbial lightning to strike. These girls figure that when they see Mr. Right, they'll just *know*. Some magical chemistry will take place and love at first sight will lead to marriage and happily ever after. Other girls figure they've got to try out all sorts of guys to see which type fits best, like tasting all the flavors at the ice cream counter before committing to just one. For them, finding their prince is just a matter of finding the right flavor, and the taste test is on like Donkey Kong. Then there are the girls who have been burned by guys and are so hurt and skeptical that they've given up on love and romance and finding decent guys altogether.

I don't think it will come as a surprise to hear that none of those methods works out very well. Finding the right guy for you is definitely doable, but you'll need to have some faith and be willing to do a whole lot of homework. Working to find love? Sounds incredibly *un*romantic, I know. But if it means finding a great guy *and* having a shot at a lasting real-world romance, I think we'd both agree the hard work would be worth it.

God's Take on Mr. (Im)Perfect

The first part of your homework is this: Find out what kind of guy you should be looking for. The old cliché "There are many fish in the sea" is true—there are a ton of guys out there (a little more than 3.5 billion to be exact-ish). So how are you going to know whether to keep your eye out for a blue tang or a grouper, a tuna or a shark? Knowing what to watch for is critical if you're going to find your guy without getting crushed.

The good news is that as a God-loving girl, you've got a head start in the process. God has given you His take on what Mr. (Im)Perfect looks like. Three cheers for divine guidance in finding love! We're going to get to His opinion in a minute, but first let's talk about why I keep adding that little "(Im)" before "Perfect."

Let's just be real here for a minute. No human being is perfect, not even the best of the best of the best. The most eligible, godly guy on the planet is still a sinner, saved only by grace, and he's going to fall miserably short of perfect on at least one thousand occasions. I'm afraid some Christian leaders and authors have done young women a disservice by focusing so much on waiting for "a godly guy" that we've allowed the bar to be set somewhere way above realistic. I sin, you sin. I have baggage, you have baggage. We can both be selfish, greedy, short-tempered, unfair, shortsighted, and just plain ugly. And guess what—so will any guy you meet, even a godly one. If you or I are looking for Mr. Perfect, we'll be looking . . . and looking . . . and looking . . . and *looking* our whole lives. But if we've got our sights set on finding Mr. (Im)Perfect—a sinful man who is set on following hard after God, perfect in his imperfections—then we've got a fighting chance at finding our Prince Charming.

Got it? Sweet. Now, let's get back to finding out what God calls a good guy.

God isn't kidding when He says He wants us to be holy—set apart and different from the world. The Bible is full of verses for both guys and girls that call us out of our me-first, obnoxious, sinful ways and point us to a higher standard of character and righteousness. In the next chapter, we're going to talk a little more about God's standards for His daughters, but let's put the guys on the chopping block first, shall we? (They can't object if they're not in on this conversation!) God has called guys to some very specific standards, and a wise girl is looking for a guy who takes God seriously enough to work on those character qualities.

God calls husbands to lead their brides (and later their children). Make a mental note (better yet, write this down): You're looking for a man who can lead. And if you're after a good leader, why not look for someone who's qualified to lead Christ's bride, the church? Paul lays out the qualifications for church leaders in 1 Timothy 3:1-10 and Titus 1:6-9 and 2:6-8. (My comments are in parentheses.) If you're after a godly leader, you're looking for someone who:

- Lives his life blamelessly and above reproach
- Is faithful to his wife (even before he is married)
- Exercises self-control (how about things like TV time, eating habits, and getting homework done?)
- Lives wisely
- Is just
- Isn't a heavy drinker (or addicted to anything else)
- Has a good reputation, even with unbelievers
- Enjoys having guests in his home (makes others feel welcome and knows how to build friendships)
- Is able to teach (knows God's Word well enough to teach it to his future wife and children)
- Is gentle
- Isn't violent, quick-tempered, or quarrelsome
- Seems like he will manage his own family well and have children who respect and obey him

- Is well respected
- Has integrity (is honest and stands up for what he believes is right)
- Doesn't love money and isn't dishonest with it
- Has a strong belief in God's teaching and is committed to the gospel
- Isn't a brand-new believer but has some spiritual depth to him
- Lives with a clear conscience (doesn't hide or ignore his sin)
- Loves what is good (for example, is what he listens to, watches, reads, and thinks about "good"?)
- Lives a devout and disciplined life (works on spiritual disciplines such as Bible reading, prayer, fellowship, and service)
- Encourages others with wholesome teaching
- Shows those who oppose the gospel where they are wrong
- Isn't arrogant (prideful)
- Is an example to others by doing all kinds of good works

I told you it was a high standard! (If you're feeling bad for the fellas right about now, don't worry; it will be our turn to get grilled in the next chapter.)

Some of those qualities are a little tough to gauge, right? How do you know whether the guy you're interested in will be able to teach the Word or have control over his kids when that's, like, *way* in the future? Proverbs 20:11 says, "Even a young man is known by his actions—if his behavior is pure and upright" (HCSB). A person's actions tell the story. If a sixteen-year-old or twenty-five-year-old guy is known to act "pure and upright," he'll probably continue to grow in purity and righteousness when he's thirty or forty or even ninety. Present character is a pretty good indicator of future character. Obviously the Holy Spirit is at work in every Christian, making us more like Jesus with each passing birthday. We're works in progress. But don't underestimate the importance of godly character today. You want to look for a guy who is modeling Christlikeness now; then there will be a really good chance that you'll have a godly leader in the distant tomorrow.

Have I mentioned that those qualifications for church leaders set the standard *really* high? You might be wondering whether there are any guys who would fit that description. Let me assure you that, yes, there are guys like this out there. They are the minority, sure, but the girl who is willing to wait for God's timing and plan for her love story won't be disappointed. Let me say again, don't expect perfection. Your Prince Charming *will* be a royal sinner! I don't want to stress "spiritual leader" so much that I backhandedly create unrealistic expectations. He might not pastor a church, rise before dawn to lead his family in devotions, or become a missionary. The character qualities in 1 Timothy 3 and Titus 1–2 are not negotiable for church leaders (they are absolutely necessary), but they're guidelines for finding a husband, not hard-and-fast rules.

The bottom line is, I want God's best for you in a future husband, and that kind of guy is going to look a whole lot like that list of qualifications. But he probably won't match it perfectly, especially when he's in his teens and twenties. Here's a rule of thumb for finding a godly guy, based on 1 Timothy 3:10: Before you decide whether a guy is worthy of your heart (someone who would be able to lead his bride in a godly way), examine him closely. If he passes the test, *then* let him pursue you.

On the Lookout

Examine him closely. It was what Paul told Timothy to do for any prospective church leader, and a wise girl "examines" her potential suitors with discernment too. No, I'm not recommending that you grill every guy you encounter like a police sergeant conducting an investigation. You're more like an undercover cop, scoping the scene for clues to his character, watching to see how he treats others, how he spends his time, and whether his actions match his words.

As you search for a potential match—and especially if you develop feelings for a contender—remember the first five of "God's Instructions for Relationships" we looked at in chapter 5:

- Treat each other like family. Until you're married, you're brothers and sisters in Christ.
- Don't get trapped. Ask yourself whether the guy or relationship you're considering would be good for you or whether you'd be limited by your affections.
- Team up with a believer. Don't even consider a relationship with someone who doesn't share your faith in God.
- Choose a godly guy. Looks, popularity, even being "nice" pale in comparison to a guy who fears and honors God.
- Honor your parents. God can use your parents to protect you from choosing a loser.

Get a handle on these guidelines because they will serve you well as you search for that solid guy (who just might be your

Prince Charming). But I've also put together a few bonus tips to help you in your search for Mr. (Im)Perfect.

Tip #1: Make a list.

When I was in college, someone suggested that I make a list of all the qualities I was looking for in a future husband. (I suspect that this person could tell by my haphazard taste in guys that I didn't have a clue what I was doing!) If you're careful not to get ultra-specific, this can be a really good tool to help you figure out what kind of guy you're looking for. By not ultra-specific, I mean that it probably won't be productive to fill your list with particulars like "listens to the same kind of music I do" or "wants to live in Hawaii someday." Dwelling on the details will exclude a whole bunch of great guys. So don't be too picky. But if you're a country girl through and through, you're probably not going to do well with a city-lovin', skinny jean–wearing, sports car–driving kind of guy, even if he *is* really cute and sweet and positively adores you. (Trust me on this one.) If you just know that living in wide open spaces is one of the keys to your happiness, then finding a guy who shares that desire would be smart. If you've always wanted to be a stay-at-home mom, you're going to want to find someone who supports that goal. Make sense?

Some of the items you place on your list will be universal if you're looking for a godly leader (like Paul's list we looked at earlier). Others will depend on your unique personality and interests. This is a really good place for the you we discovered in chapter 3 to shine through. But let me emphasize one more time that this list is meant to be merely a guide to help you find your guy; it's not the Holy Bible. Don't get legalistic about finding someone who fits every single item you wrote down. Let me give you a personal example to help you see what I mean.

When I was in high school and college, I felt a strong sense that I wanted to serve God overseas someday as a missionary. I wouldn't say that God specifically called me to it, and I never made a vow to the Lord over it or anything; I just had a strong desire to do it. I had already traveled a lot and loved experiencing other cultures. When I coupled that with my love for God and my desire to reach the lost and dying with the good news, missionary work just seemed to be the logical choice.

Then came Paul—the handsome friend-turned-more who took me by surprise and swept me off my feet. He seemed like a great match for me on so many levels. I mean, he checked off nearly all my little "Husband Wish List" boxes. However, he made it very clear that he did not feel God calling him to be a missionary. He really had no desire to even *travel* overseas at the time. I took a good look at him and then a good look at my list, and I was totally confused! I clearly remember a conversation I had with a godly woman (who happened to be a missionary's wife) around that same time. Debbie gave me some great advice. She said, "Once you get married, loving and serving your husband and family becomes your primary ministry, whether you're in the United States or another country. So find a man whom you can joyfully serve and do ministry alongside no matter where you end up living." Solid advice, right? (Let me just give a quick plug for surrounding yourself with godly older women who can set you straight from time to time!)

After that talk, and after much more prayer, I realized that Paul's desire to serve God right here in North America wasn't a deal breaker. Even though it didn't fit my "list," I could let it go. The essence of that amazing man trumped a little tally box on a piece of paper. (And the irony is that I *have* been able to serve God overseas after all. Through that little thing called the Internet, I've been able to mentor girls from literally all over the world! God makes me smile.)

So make your list. Check it twice. Then ask God to give you wisdom to see which of those items are essential and which you can erase if the right guy comes along.

Tip #2: Keep your eyes wide open.

I'm sure you've heard the phrase "Love is blind." I beg to differ. Boy, do I beg to differ! Yes, once you're married, you should exercise the grace of 1 Corinthians 13 love, but until there's a ring on your finger, girl, your eyes should be *wide* open! Don't let the butterflies and the flattery of having a guy fawn over you keep you from seeing who he really is.

Just like you're on the lookout for a guy with great qualities, you're also on the hunt to scope out any potential problems once you think you've found him. Part of your homework in finding Mr. (Im)Perfect is to look for red flags. Red flags mean stop, do not pass go, do not go any further in this relationship until you get answers. Proverbs 27:12 says, "A prudent person foresees danger and takes precautions. The simpleton goes blindly on and suffers the consequences." Look for potential signs of danger—sexual pressure, anger issues, jealousy, disregard for God—and take cover if you see them! According to this verse, only foolish girls keep going in a relationship when they see those red flags (hoping he'll change), and they end up getting punished for their wishful thinking. You're smart. Stay out (or get out) of the relationship if you see red flags, and save yourself a whole lot of heartache.

Another part of keeping your eyes open is being realistic. Statistically speaking, relationships don't last very long in high school and college. Wise girls realize this and don't get so carried away with their emotions that they forget reason. Wise girls also listen to the advice of their parents, mentors, and godly friends and weigh it carefully. They don't let their growing love blind them to the truth.

Tip #3: Be friends.

This tip is easier when you have a handle on one of God's instructions for relationships that we looked at in chapter 5: Treat your brothers in Christ like brothers. Get to know guys as friends before you consider being anything more. It just makes sense, doesn't it? The best marriage relationships start out as friendships. Mine did. I tell you, it works! Don't rush to get to the romance. Savor the opportunity to learn about any guy you're interested in while just being friends. (And I mean *real* friends, not "friends with benefits.") My husband will be the first to tell you that once a guy is interested in you, he will put on a good show to try to win your heart. So your best chance of seeing the "real him" is before that point, while you're just friends.

While you're hanging out with your guy friends, watch them. Learn what makes them tick. (In the spirit of full disclosure, I'm not *entirely* sure that's humanly possible.) If you're looking for a godly leader, watch your guy friends to see what that looks like (or *doesn't* look like) in the real world. Consider all the guys in your world as case studies, living examples of the qualities you do and don't want in a future husband. I guess I should add here that it helps to spend time with quality guy friends—the kind of guys who are going to show you what a gentleman looks like.

Speaking of gentlemen, part of your job as a sister is to help the guys in your life become them. Sometimes you've just got to help a brother out! Not all guys get that training at home, so teach your brothers how to treat a lady by being one when you're around them. (If you're more of a tomboy, don't sweat it. I'm not saying you can't shoot hoops with the guys. But even if you *can* outshoot them, you still have a responsibility to help them understand how to treat a girl right.) Let your guy friends look after you, even if you're perfectly capable of looking out for yourself. Let them open doors for you, and don't let them talk to you like "one of the guys." Even if you don't end up marrying one of them, at least you've helped an unknown sister by training *her* future husband to be a gentleman.

Tip #4: Make him prove himself.

Like my husband is quick to warn, guys are really good at *acting* godly and nice and all that when they're on the chase for their gal. He tells the story of one of his friends who was completely fooled by a guy she had fallen for. Her boyfriend convinced her that he loved God and was the one for her, and they were married not long after. But once the wedding bells stopped ringing, his true self shone through. He had never been a Christian and had no intention of living life God's way. He had bluffed his way through the whole thing, and she was left with the prospect of a lifetime with this jerk.

I don't share that story to scare you but rather to emphasize the importance of making a guy prove himself to you. It takes time. Your guy might be able to spout all sorts of flowery, sweet promises. He might even go to church and claim to love God. But time will tell whether he's genuine. Jesus taught that the way to know a person's true character is to look at the fruit in his or her life (see Luke 6:44), and fruit takes time to grow.

The quest for your heart should take some effort on his part. If a guy is after your heart, make him pursue it. Girls often make it too easy for guys (I was so guilty of that!). I've spent quite a bit of time thinking about why we do it, why we bend over backward to make ourselves overly available. Maybe we don't feel that we're worth being pursued. We have such a low opinion of ourselves that we want to make it as easy as possible for the guy so he won't lose interest and leave. This way of thinking is unhealthy. In fact, it'll backfire on you. Why? Because God designed guys to pursue us, not the other way around.

If you make it obvious to a guy that you're head over heels for him (by flirting, sending him a gazillion texts, telling your friends to "accidentally" mention that you like him), a quality guy is going to back off big-time. A guy isn't forced to respect and honor a girl who fawns over him because he doesn't have to work for her affection. I'm not talking about playing hard to get, like it's some sort of game. I *am* talking about having some respect for yourself and understanding that you are worth the effort it will take for a guy to pursue you. Let him show you that you're worth the endeavor!

I was so impatient and headstrong that I ended up scaring off more than one quality guy. It wasn't pretty. We're talking flirting, calling, making plans—I even wrote a poem to get a guy to notice me once. (I know. Desperate, right?) It took me a long time to figure out I needed to have more self-respect and wait for a guy who would think, *Wow, that Jessie is something else. I think*

I want to get to know her better. Eventually I focused on keeping my eyes on Christ and stopped chasing boys. When the time was right, God did in fact bring me my very own Mr. (Im)Perfect—a man who respects, values, and *still* pursues me.

So make him prove himself. Wait patiently for a man who appreciates all that you are. Don't settle for less than you deserve just to get what you want.

The Search

It was New Year's Day, and Yosemite National Park was quiet under a thick blanket of fresh snow. Paul and I had visited the park every New Year's Day since he proposed to me there on January 1, 2002, and this particular visit was shaping up to be just as perfect as the rest. My hubby takes amazing landscape photography, so we spent the day photo-hopping around the park. Yosemite Falls, Half Dome, El Capitan, the quaint little church—we hit all the good spots, and he got some great shots. Near the end of the day, we stopped at Curry Village to get some snacks and warm up a bit. That's when he noticed it. His wedding ring. *It was gone.*

He checked his pockets, his camera gear, the inside of his gloves, and between the car seats. We traced our steps around the village, hoping it had fallen off his hand somewhere close by. The alternative was depressing. If he had lost it while taking photos, it could be anywhere. We'd wound our way along miles of roads and trails, all—don't forget—covered in snow. When we finally quit searching the village, we pretty much gave up hope of finding his ring. Losing his wedding ring on the anniversary of our engagement, at the same location where he asked me to marry him, was ironic (in a sad way). We didn't want to give up, but looking out over that vast Yosemite Valley, the impossibility of ever finding his ring sobered us, and we packed up to head home.

Before we left the park, Paul asked if he could make one last stop. Now that the afternoon sun was casting better lighting, he wanted to retake photos at the very first location he had shot that morning. So we parked the car, he ran off down the trail to do his magic, and I trailed along behind, praying as I went: *Lord, I know it's just a wedding ring and that in light of eternity it doesn't matter all that much. But it's special to us, and I know that You know exactly where it is. We've looked and looked with no luck, but if You'd let us find it, we will always remember every January first that You are a God who does miracles.* I finished my prayer just as I reached the overlook. I looked down at my feet, and—I'm not making this up!—there, making a perfect silver circle in the snow, was Paul's wedding ring.

Even writing it now, I'm grinning from ear to ear, tears glistening in my eyes, remembering all over again the giddy excitement that filled my heart in that instant. God reached into space and time and did for me what I could *never* do on my own. We serve a God who works miracles! The God who spoke this universe into existence, who holds the stars and planets in place and needs absolutely nothing from you, chooses to love you, pursue you, and give you everything you need. This same God is perfectly able to do anything. He "is able . . . to accomplish infinitely more than we might ask or think" (Ephesians 3:20).

Does finding a godly man who will cherish, love, and lead you feel impossible? Maybe it is—for you. But leading you to your husband is child's play for your God! I can promise you this: If marriage is what is best for you, God will deliver. Your job is to trust Him, wait for His timing, do your homework, and then focus on becoming the kind of woman a godly guy will be attracted to. (We'll get to that next.)

> *Father, I know You delight to give good gifts to Your children. I also know that if You can create this whole universe with a word, You can certainly handle leading me to a man who loves You and whom I can serve You alongside. I'm so eager as I wait for the day You'll show him to me, but in the meantime, help my eyes to see clearly, my heart to remain steady, and my soul to feast on You while I wait for my Mr. (Im)Perfect. Amen.*

Discussion Questions

1. What are some qualities you plan to look for in a guy?

2. Why is it important that a potential husband be able to lead?

3. What negative qualities ("red flags") should you watch out for in a guy?

4. Why is it important to make a guy prove his character over time?

5. What does it mean to let a guy pursue you instead of the other way around? Why is that important?

CHAPTER 7

Becoming Miss (Im)Perfect

The other day, Paul e-mailed me an article titled "11 Reasons Men Love Women." Under the link to the article he wrote, "See? Now you'll believe me!" with a little smiley face. As I read the article, I was shocked to find that there are, in fact, other guys on this planet who have the same strange view of beauty my husband has. Who knew? Number one in the article read,

1. Your sweaty post-gym rawness
You think you're most desirable when you're all dolled up and looking as elegant as a champagne flute. No. It's at 6 o'clock on a weekday, when you're just back from the gym in an old gray tank top and a sports bra, devoid of makeup and perfume—when you are nothing but raw, glistening, briny womanness. "Ewww," you say, "I'm so gross!" We so beg to differ.[8]

Now, I hate to admit when I'm wrong, but this time I had no choice. I had been absolutely convinced that my husband was the only guy who could possibly feel that way, but evidence to the contrary was staring me in the face. "Raw, glistening, briny womanness" is attractive to most guys? Really?

There's something to be said for getting dressed up and looking "as elegant as a champagne flute" every once in a while, but apparently guys dig it even more when we're just *us*—free from all the fuss and fluff and stuff we paste on ourselves, trying to become the attractive girls we already are in their eyes. Funny, isn't it? I really do get home from the gym all sweaty, with no makeup and smelling like I've been camping for a few days, and the first words out of Paul's mouth are, "Well, look at you, cutie." I can't help but roll my eyes. He can't be serious, can he? I'm trying to get to the shower before he realizes just how gross I am, and he's looking at me like I'm the most beautiful thing he's ever laid eyes on.

We've been married more than a decade, and I still don't completely understand why his idea of beauty is so different from mine. But as that article proved, Paul isn't alone. Guys have a very different idea about beauty and what's attractive than we do! While we girls are busy looking to magazines, movies, and models to find out what a guy wants, we've totally missed the memo about what guys *really* desire in a woman. Maybe we should start taking our cue from somewhere else—hmmm, like God's Word?—to find the ideal. Why not? If a godly girl looks in the Bible to find the standard for her future husband, wouldn't it make sense that a godly guy is looking there too? How else will he know what he should be looking for in a wife?

Lessons from a Tackle Shop

Stanley, Idaho, is a quaint little mountain town with a population that could fit on a small commuter jet. It's *that* small.

The dirt streets and old-fashioned buildings give you the feeling you're stepping back in time and starring in an old western movie. There aren't a whole lot of reasons to vacation there unless you're gaga for pristine, jaw-droppingly gorgeous, towering mountain awesomeness (which Paul and I are). Because Stanley is nestled at the base of the immense, snow-capped Sawtooth Mountains, it became the perfect base camp for one of our backpacking trips.

Before we could hit the trail, I was in serious need of some bug repellent. (The mosquitoes in that part of the country could suck an elephant dry in thirty seconds flat.) There aren't many shopping options in Stanley, so I made my way to the "tackle and gift shop." For such a small town, they don't mess around when it comes to fishing tackle. They had an entire wall filled with lures—some feathery, some glittery, some neon colored and rubbery, and some that would have made really cute earrings! While I was looking for the kills-every-bug-in-sight spray (I'm talking 100 percent DEET, baby), I overheard the shopkeeper helping a customer. Apparently, the guy was a fisherman, and he was looking to catch a very particular kind of fish. I don't remember what kind of fish it was (probably some kind of trout). It doesn't really matter. The point is that out of those hundreds of fishing lures, the shopkeeper pointed out the exact one that would attract the kind of fish this guy was after.

Humor me for a second and consider that landing a godly guy is a lot like fishing in an alpine lake. You know what kind of guy you're looking to "catch." You read that profile in chapter 6. Now you need the right "bait" (and the patience of a seasoned fisherman!) if you're going to catch him.

I'm sure someone out there will get offended that I'm calling guys "fish" and girls "bait" and all that. Trust me, I'm not creating doctrine out of this or anything. It's just an analogy. You have to admit, though, that there's some truth to the comparison. The kind of bait we use as girls is going to attract *someone*, so you might as well make sure your lure matches the kind of guy you want to catch.

First rule of fishing: If you're looking for a godly guy, you're going to have to become a godly girl.

God's Take on Miss (Im)Perfect

In the previous chapter, we saw just how high God sets the standard for men who want to lead in the church and, subsequently, those who desire to lead any of His beautiful daughters. Now it's our turn, ladies. God's standards for a godly woman are no less important, and no less intimidating! But there's a tremendous freedom in actually having the right standard for femininity instead of chasing after some airbrushed, unrealistic ideal our whole lives. I'd rather know the truth about God's standards for me than be in the dark, even if it means I have to change my views on some things, and even if it means a whole lot of hard work. Wouldn't you?

But first, let's talk about that little "(Im)" again. Before we look at God's ideal for wives, I want you to take a deep breath and say it with me: "I am never going to be perfect this side of eternity." Got it? You're not perfect, and you never will be as long as you live in a fallen world. We girls can be really hard on ourselves! This discussion isn't meant to discourage you or make you feel like you'll never measure up and nobody will ever want a big mess-up like you. No way!

As we look at God's design for womanhood, we should get *excited* about all He has planned for our lives and how our design glorifies Him. I want you to find freedom from the world's twisted ideas about beauty and how a girl should act and dress and talk, and I want you to find joy and happiness in being the *you* God intends you to be. So don't get discouraged if you feel like you have a long way to go to become the solid counterpart to a godly guy. That's what the Holy Spirit is for, right? To show us where we're wrong and lead us into truth! God knew I had a *loooong* way to go. I still do! But we serve a faithful God, and none of us is alone on that journey.

Now, what does God's Word have to say about becoming a godly, desirable woman?

Most of the commands God gives in the Bible about character are universal to both guys and girls. For example, God's not gender specific when He tells us to "[care] for orphans and widows" (James 1:27), "to do what is right, to love mercy, and to walk humbly with [Him]" (Micah 6:8), and to "be holy in everything [we] do" (1 Peter 1:15). You'd be wise to get to know those commands (read: get familiar with your Bible!). But there is one somewhat famous passage of Scripture specifically written to help young men know what to look for in a woman. It's like the CliffsNotes for guys when it comes to finding "the one," so you really should get to know this section of your Bible.

Proverbs 31:10-31 is a Hebrew poem, originally told by a queen to her son. This wise momma wanted her son, Lemuel, to make a smart choice in a bride instead of going with the most common male mate-selection process, which is to look for the hottest, most enchanting girl you can find and make her yours at all costs. She specifically warned against that model. She said,

"Charm is deceptive, and beauty does not last," so look for a woman "who fears the LORD" (see verse 30). Here's a list of the other qualities the Queen Mother advised her son to look for if he wanted a wife "more precious than rubies" (verse 10), plus a few bonus qualities from other Bible passages.

A God-fearing guy should look for a woman who:

- Is virtuous (has high morals and lives by them)
- Is capable
- Is trustworthy
- Will greatly enrich his life
- Will bring him good, not harm, all the days of her life
- Is a hard worker, not lazy
- Takes care of the people in her life
- Is wise with money
- Is energetic
- Is strong
- Helps the poor and needy
- Plans ahead
- Dresses with dignity
- Laughs instead of freaking out
- Doesn't worry about the future
- Speaks wisely and with kindness
- Fears God
- Doesn't have to brag, as her actions speak for themselves
- Would be willing to leave her family and friends to follow her husband wherever the Lord takes them (see Psalm 45:10)
- Doesn't quarrel or complain (see Proverbs 21:19)
- Has a gentle and quiet spirit (see 1 Peter 3:4)

- Will respect and submit to her husband (see Ephesians 5:22,33)

Don't feel so bad for the guys anymore? Sheesh—we have our own work cut out for us! But it's good work, right? Remember, God doesn't give us instructions just for the fun of it. He gives us guidelines for living because He knows exactly what it takes to have a genuinely happy life. God knows what will bring Him the most glory—which attitudes in us will make Him look good. And let's face it, any girl who can live out that list will be a living billboard proclaiming, "There *is* a God!"

If you're still a teenager or if you're in your twenties with no prospects of marriage anytime soon, you might be tempted to write this list off as a "someday" kind of thing. Let's take another look at Proverbs 20:11, this time for ourselves: "Even a young [woman] is known by [her] actions—if [her] behavior is pure and upright" (HCSB). Gut check: Are you known to act "pure and upright" today? Are you trustworthy, hardworking, and wise? Do you laugh at uncertainty or freak out? Do you fear God? Remember, present character is a pretty good indicator of future character. Are you on the right track? Are you becoming the kind of girl who is going to attract the kind of guy you're hoping for?

The Perfect Bait

Let's go back to the bait. When you look around at your fellow female-folk, how would you say they "display" themselves? What kind of bait are they throwing out into the lake of life in the hopes of catching a guy? How do the girls you know dress, carry themselves, and talk? How do they interact with guys? What messages and pictures do they share on social media?

How about you?

It's easy to see the wrong bait all around us. It doesn't take a doctoral degree to see that if a girl flaunts her body and messes around, she isn't going to land a stellar guy. So rather than spend a lot of time talking about all the ridiculous ways many girls try to attract members of the opposite sex, let's just focus on three great and really attractive qualities largely missing from girls' repertoires these days: dignity, modesty, and mystery.

Dignity, modesty, and mystery—each one is a force to be reckoned with. But the combination of this threefold powerhouse packs a serious punch. A girl with dignity, modesty, and mystery displays strength under control, concern for those around her, and trust that God is in control of her love life. A girl with these three qualities is, well, one of the most beautiful things God has created on this earth! So what does this marvel of femininity look like in everyday life?

Dignity

By definition, a girl with dignity lives in a way that is worthy of honor, respect, and admiration. She lives that way because she has respect for herself. Why does she have respect for herself? Track with me—this is the really important part. A girl with dignity has respect for herself because she knows her worth. She holds her head high (even if no one knows her name, even if she gets bullied or looked down on or made fun of) because she understands that her worth isn't based on others' opinions. Instead, a girl with true dignity knows that her worth is based on who she is in Christ—who she is as God's daughter. And here's what your Daddy says about you:

- He made you in His image (see Genesis 1:27). That's a crazy-good mold to come from!
- He said that creating girls was a very good thing (see Genesis 1:31). Can I get an amen?
- He personally designed you from top to bottom. He knows every little detail about your design, and He thinks He did a fabulous job (see Psalm 139:13-16).
- You are beautiful and bring Him pleasure (see Song of Songs 7:6).
- He delights in you so much that He sings over you (see Zephaniah 3:17).

Those are some pretty good reasons to hold your head high! Think of it this way: You have to choose whether you're going to view yourself as the real deal or an imitation, as a crystal glass or a Styrofoam cup. What does that have to do with catching a godly guy? Why is it important for you to decide? Because if you believe the truth—that you are a beautiful treasure, like a crystal glass—then you're going to protect your heart. If you believe you are valuable, then you're going to wait for someone who understands the treasure you are. But if you view yourself as a Styrofoam cup—something to be used and thrown away—then you're not going to object if a guy treats you like you're disposable. You'll expect it.

So which is it? Are you going to accept that you are a precious, beautiful daughter of the King, or are you going to insist on seeing yourself as trash? Are you going to hold your head high in dignity and live like the princess you are, or are you going to allow others to use and disregard you?

Dignity is a heart attitude that becomes a lifestyle. When you understand the truth of who you are—when you *really* believe it—then every aspect of your life will follow suit, from your clothes to your text messages. Dignity comes first, and then come the next two qualities of an irresistible girl: modesty and mystery.

Modesty

I'm afraid that for some of us, the word *modesty* conjures up images of calico prairie dresses and drab hair. It's too bad, really. The media has given modesty a really bad rap, but you don't have to choose between modesty and style. Truly. It's not that hard to find clothes that cover the places that should remain private; you just have to *want* to find them. And let me tell you why it's important to go through the effort—and, yes, sometimes sacrifice—to dress modestly. We're talking about bait, remember? What you wear is the flashiest part of your tackle. It's the first thing a guy sees when he looks at you. Don't underestimate the ability of your clothing to either attract or repel the guy you're after.

So if you're looking for a quality guy, might I suggest you dress the part? We're talking classy, not trashy.[9] Think about the leader we envisioned together in chapter 6. Do you think that kind of guy would want his future wife flaunting her body for all the other guys to see? Nope. Think he'd be keen on her wearing shorts that barely count as underwear, or shirts that show her bra underneath? No way. Think he'd want her sporting the panties I saw at American Eagle that read, "I Only Ride Big Waves" and "I Got Leid in Hawaii"? Fat chance. If you want to kill your dignity and attract creepers, then go for broke and wear next to nothing or clothes with suggestive messages. But if you want to attract a godly guy, then dress in a way that is going to keep guys looking you in the eyes, not scanning you up and down like a piece of meat. Let's dress like we're saving our body for the man who is going to cherish it forever, okay?

By the way, modesty is more than clothes on skin. How can a girl convey modesty in the way she acts around guys? How about in the way she talks (in person and online)? Here's one we don't think about too often, but how can a girl's body language show modesty?

There's a delicate power in modesty, and it has to do with mystery, the third quality in "the perfect bait."

Mystery

The other night, Paul rented a movie called *The Impossible* for us to watch after the kids went to bed. The movie followed a family of five who were vacationing in the Philippines when the 2004 Indian Ocean tsunami hit. I had purposefully avoided reading any reviews about the story before we watched the movie because I'm a sucker for a good mystery. I love being carried along with the narrative. So, not knowing what would happen to this family (a mom, a dad, and three young boys), I was gripped by emotion as the tsunami tore the family from one another. *Would they survive? Would they find each other?* I was near tears as the camera followed the mother, swept along by the tower of water, battered by floating debris, just trying to keep her head above water.

It was in this swelling roller coaster of emotion that the love of my life leaned over and said matter-of-factly, "Man, I can't believe she survived all that."

I looked at him and gave him my most teenagery eye roll. "Paulieeeee! I can't believe you just ruined it!"

"What? Ah . . . oh . . . I thought you knew!" he stammered.

The good news is that after a few months of counseling, I did forgive my husband for giving away the end of the movie, and we're friends again.

We all love a good mystery, right? We don't want to know the end at the beginning! Whether we're watching a movie or getting to know someone, we want to be led on a journey to that aha moment when we can finally see the whole picture.

A girl with mystery leaves room for discovery, both emotional and physical.

What does that look like, practically speaking? A girl with mystery doesn't bare all to everyone. That includes not baring her body (which we've already talked about), but mystery is more than physical. Being mysterious means that you save some surprises about yourself and your feelings for later; you don't share everything about you and all your hopes and dreams for a relationship and life ever after on a first date. As a guy pursues you, then you can allow him to come on that journey of discovery into who you are. You can let him get to know you, bit by bit, wonderful surprise by wonderful surprise.

When a girl is mysterious, it forces a guy to be a man. It forces him to get up the courage to pursue you. And you *want* a guy who can lead, remember? There's no opportunity for a guy to show his character if you've already hinted—or flat-out told him—that you're crazy about him and he can have you if he wants you. Does that make sense? A girl with mystery doesn't play games, but she doesn't make it too easy on a potential husband either. She makes sure any guy who wants her heart is ready to prove, over time, that he's willing to go to the ends of the earth for it because she is *that* precious to him.

The Ultimate Goal

Let me take a step back and clarify one thing: The point of godly character isn't just to catch a godly guy. The last thing I'm suggesting is that you should pursue godliness just so you can attract a prime member of the opposite sex! The point of becoming more like Jesus Christ is to enjoy the rich fullness of a relationship with God. It's just an added bonus that godliness and internal beauty are also really attractive to a godly guy. The ultimate goal of godliness *is* godliness, not a better relationship status.

Pursuing godliness is a win-win for you. If you focus on becoming more like Christ, you're going to attract the right kind of guy. But if you focus on becoming more like Christ, and God asks you to wait a while (or if He says no to marriage altogether), guess what? You'll still be more like Christ, which is the whole point of our existence on this planet: to know God and make Him known to others. Like I said, pursuing godly character is a win-win. As long as you're following hard after God, you'll be blessed if you find Mr. (Im)Perfect and blessed if you don't.

Matthew 5:6 says, "Those who hunger and thirst for righteousness . . . will be filled" (HCSB). On the other hand, when we hunger and thirst for a guy, we'll be disappointed every time. Worse yet, we'll get our hearts crushed. Remember chapter 2? Only God can fill us; only He can make us whole. Let's hunger and thirst after Him alone, trusting that if the right fish is out there, at least we've got the proper bait on the line.

So go ahead and be you. Work on your shortcomings, work at showing the godliness inside your heart to those around you, and see what God does. Finding your match may take time, but

I have a feeling some lucky guy is going to be head over heels for his very own Miss (Im)Perfect in God's perfect timing.

> *Holy God, I know that You want me to be more like Your Son, Jesus. That's what I want too. I fall short so often and in so many ways, but I want to keep growing. You know that I want to keep growing. Help me to keep my eyes focused on that goal instead of obsessing over guys and what they think of me. I trust that as I "hunger and thirst for righteousness," You will take care of the matchmaking. Thank You for being my biggest advocate, Daddy. Amen.*

Discussion Questions

1. *If you want to catch a godly guy, what kind of "bait" are you going to have to use?*

2. *What qualities will a godly guy be looking for in a wife?*

3. *What is dignity? How does an attitude of dignity become a lifestyle?*

4. *Think about the way you dress. What type of guy are you likely to attract? Are you happy with that prospect?*

5. *What do you think it means for a girl to remain mysterious? Can you think of any other practical ways a girl can leave room for discovery?*

6. *What is the ultimate goal of godly character? (Hint: It's not just to catch a great guy!)*

7. *Pull out your journal and write a prayer to God, asking Him to show you the places in your life where you need to grow in Christlike character.*

CHAPTER 8

Respect the Fire and You Won't Get Burned

When it comes to purity, I have known failure and I have known success. Because of those successes, I know it is, in fact, possible to find your guy without getting crushed by compromise, and my life's mission is to help you see how.

In a moment of insecurity, one day I asked God why He chose me—with all my miserably failed attempts at purity—to be a spokesperson for it. He gently reminded me that it is because of those failed attempts that my heart is so passionate about preserving *your* purity! I know the devastation of sin, how it darkens your world and separates you from God. And I know the exhilarating freedom of a clear conscience before God. My hope is that as you read this chapter, you won't see a list of dos and don'ts. My hope is that you won't be gripped by fear of failure or buried under a heap of shame if you've already compromised. My hope is that you will be inspired and empowered by God's take on sexual purity. There is freedom whenever we follow God's way of living! And there is joy and hope and pride and beauty when you take your purity seriously.

The Nature of Intimacy

As the title suggests, the core message of this book is that you don't have to let guys make or break you. And the number one way a girl allows her heart to be crushed by her crush is when she gives him access to her body, only to have him walk away. Why is that? Why does physical stuff have such a profound effect on our hearts?

When God made the first man and the first woman, He gave them hormones and body parts and all those things you learned about in sex ed way back in middle school. But what your sex ed teacher probably *didn't* tell you is that sex is more than just the act of penetration and procreation. (Thanks to you, middle school health teacher, I will forever despise those words.) God made humans way more complex than animals. He didn't design us just to make babies but to be "united into one." Genesis 2:24 says,

> A man leaves his father and mother and is joined to his wife, and the two are united into one.

How exactly are two people "united into one"? Paul clarifies it for us in 1 Corinthians 6:16:

> There's more to sex than mere skin on skin. Sex is as much spiritual mystery as physical fact. As written in Scripture, "The two become one." (MSG)

A man and woman "become one" by both the physical and spiritual dimensions of intimacy. Sex solidifies people. It's like relationship cement. Scientists are now finding all sorts of evidence for this—how neurochemicals react in the brain, causing a guy and a girl to be intensely connected to each other following intimacy.[10] (Don't you love how science always comes around to what God already said ages ago?)

Jesus said, "Since they are no longer two but one, let no one split apart what God has joined together" (Matthew 19:6). God's design is for one man and one woman for life. When we cement ourselves to guys through physical intimacy before marriage, we risk getting our hearts ripped apart by the separation. It's not pretty (or painless). In fact, that's one of the reasons a breakup is like divorce. If you were physically intimate with your boyfriend, when you broke up, you separated what God had joined together.

Pretty heavy stuff, right?

That's why the Bible is so clear and so strong on the subject of physical purity:

> Run from sexual sin! No other sin so clearly affects the
> body as this one does. For sexual immorality is a sin
> against your own body. Don't you realize that your body
> is the temple of the Holy Spirit, who lives in you and
> was given to you by God? You do not belong to yourself,
> for God bought you with a high price. So you must
> honor God with your body. (1 CORINTHIANS 6:18-20)

God designed sexual intimacy to join together two people, but He intends the cement to be laid *after* marriage. That begs a question I hear all the time: *How far is too far?* In other words, *Just how far can I go before the cement starts hardening?*

Tripping over "The Line"

I remember wanting to know the answer to that question too. I wanted to know just how far I could go with a guy and still be "safe," because I loved God and really did want to stay pure for Him. I wanted to know where that infamous line was, and I was convinced that once I knew where it was, I wouldn't cross it.

I scoured books, and I listened to pastors speak on the topic. I journaled and I prayed. I honestly don't know whether they didn't *give* the answer or I just didn't want to *hear* it. One way or another, I was so preoccupied with looking for that blasted line that I tripped right over it. I was so focused on the specifics—exactly what I could and couldn't do and still be safe—that I completely failed to see the bigger picture.

Asking, *How far is too far?* is like standing at the top of a high cliff, inching your way forward, wondering, *Just how close can I get to the edge without falling off?* That would be crazy-stupid! All it takes is one unplanned rock to crumble under your foot and you're tumbling headlong down a ravine. If you find yourself near a cliff, the smart question to ask yourself is *How far back can I stand and still enjoy the view?*

So instead of deliberating for hours over whether that stupid line should be drawn at a closed-mouth kiss or a clothes-on make-out session, let's start asking the *right* questions. I'm talking about questions like "How can I show God I take my job as His temple seriously?" and "How can I honor my husband *today?*" Because in the big picture, God's glory is more important than your temporary pleasure or pleasing your boyfriend. And in the big picture, *all* of you is meant for your husband, even before your wedding night. The right questions are important because they keep you from naively inching your way toward the edge of that cliff. The right questions keep you focused on the benefits of purity instead of on the deprivation, on the big picture instead of on nitpicky details.

What—No Kiss?

Have you seen the 2005 film version of Jane Austen's *Pride and Prejudice*? I hope so, because if you haven't, I'm going to totally ruin the end for you in a minute, and then I'm going to feel terrible and look like a complete hypocrite because I've already rattled on and on about not spoiling the end of movies and all that. So please just forgive me now.

If you have seen the movie, picture with me Miss Elizabeth Bennet, looking pale and thoughtful in the predawn morning light, thinking about the unlikely man she has grown to love over the course of an hour and a half of movie time. But she believes she has ruined her chances with him completely, so now she's out in the cold (for no apparent reason). But then— behold!—here comes the dashing Mr. Darcy, tromping through the English countryside in . . . are those his pajamas? Hard to tell. But here he comes, in his strangely stylish overcoat and his perfectly unkempt hair blowing, just a little, in the breeze. It's the moment we've all been waiting for! He strides up to Lizzy and confesses his love just as the morning sun peaks over the horizon. He bends down and their foreheads touch, and we all know what's going to happen next: love's first kiss, right?

Wrong.

He doesn't kiss her. They hold each other's hands and say some nice things, and then the scene ends. Now for those trained in the art of the Hollywood movie, this is like whiplash. We were all on the edge of our seats waiting for the obvious kissable moment! The lack of lip touch was noticeable. And when that first kiss finally did come between the pair—get this!— *after* they were married, I got to thinking . . .

Why have we allowed Hollywood to convince us that a kiss is just the logical next step after a guy and a girl have mutual feelings for each other? Brace yourself for my next thought: If all of me is meant for my future husband, wouldn't that necessarily include my lips? A countercultural question, I know.

I can't tell you how many girls have shared with me, rather embarrassed, that they haven't been kissed. Why would they be embarrassed about something as cool as that? Because society has convinced us girls that if we haven't been kissed, then we must not be desirable. Talk about faulty reasoning. Can we just get rid of that way of thinking right now? Please? Contrary to pop culture (and, coincidentally, most boyfriends), a kiss is a big deal! It shouldn't be taken lightly. Why? Because it's a gesture of physical intimacy. In other words, it's one of the first layers of relationship cement laid between two people. You don't want to be connected in that way with just anyone.

I realize that probably sounds incredibly overreactive—maybe even a little bit prudish—but hang with me for a minute. Up until the past hundred years—that is, for thousands and thousands of years—everyone accepted that a kiss was a big deal. And kissing in public was a *really* big deal, especially in biblical culture. (That's why King Solomon's bride-to-be laments the fact that she can't give him a kiss in public. See Song of Solomon 8:1.) It's only in this modern age that getting kissed by a guy is considered a normal rite of passage for a girl of any age. But it shouldn't come as a big surprise that God's not very concerned about cultural norms. He wants us to be holy, remember? His children are called to be different from the world.

WHAT'S IN A KISS? (A GUY'S POINT OF VIEW)
By Paul Minassian

What's in a kiss? A lot more than you'd think.

Guys are funny creatures. We can have the best of the best intentions, be the godliest of godly, be the most noble and all that, but wow, when we kiss a girl, all bets are off.

When a guy kisses a girl, it starts a type of "mechanism" within him. Kind of like the "click-click-click" when a roller-coaster car starts climbing up a huge incline, with a highly anticipated ten-story drop just up and over the rise. Yeah, we try to deny it. We say we don't want to go any further. But the magic potion has already kicked in, and that "click-click-click" is the hypnotic song of a thousand sirens. Put simply, once we are granted a first kiss, we immediately want the second. Here's what I mean . . .

A girl and a guy are walking, holding hands, enjoying a wonderful time together. They stop, pause, look into each other's eyes, smile, and kiss. I'd venture to say that at that point, the girl kisses the guy because she feels close to him and wants to show intimacy. After that kiss, I bet she can look into the guy's eyes, smile at him, hold his hand, and keep walking, feeling that all is right with the world. A guy is different. He might kiss the girl because he, too, feels close to her and wants to show intimacy. But once he kisses her—"click-click-click"—his mind is already thinking about the second kiss. And then the third. And then the fourth. So when the girl looks into the guy's eyes and grabs hold of his hand and is at that point quite content with continuing their walk, the guy is still looking at her lips. Well, he's looking at her eyes, then her lips, then her eyes, then her lips, and so on and so forth. Did I mention the fifth kiss yet? Or the sixth?

A noble guy might be able to employ self-control to combat the desire for more. But don't think for a moment that a guy's noble self-control (which all humans are capable of exercising) means he doesn't want the next kiss. This isn't about self-control; it's about that mechanism within us guys. "Click-click-click." It's intoxicating.

Yeah, we guys sure are funny creatures. Like panda bears: cute (and a little slow) but positively dangerous. So guard those kisses carefully.

======

Rules for Love?

I'm going to go ahead and admit it up front: At first glance, the idea of having rules for love sounds incredibly unromantic. Maybe I'm still getting over years of Hollywood chick-flick brainwashing. I don't know. There's part of me that wants love to be free and untamable. Maybe you're right there with me. But let's think about the alternative for a minute. What if love actually *did* have a mind of its own? What if you couldn't control romance, emotion, and desire any more than you could control wind and fire? If love defied rules, we humans would be at the mercy of some mystical connection and our hormones (a scary combination). That doesn't sound like it would end very well, does it?

"Rules," "boundaries," "guidelines"—whatever you want to call them, God knows just what a mess we would make of our lives if we didn't have them. He knows exactly how fast a connection can sizzle between two people. He gave us the ability and desire to "become one flesh," remember? If we didn't have guidelines to keep us in check, we'd go around unknowingly cementing ourselves to guy after guy, only to be ripped apart when the relationship ends. Which is a lot of pain. And not any fun. (As some of us, sadly, already know.) In this case, rules are actually at the heart of our freedom. Did you catch that? God's rules for the physical aspect of a relationship *safeguard* your freedom! They keep you from getting trapped.

I'm not here to make up rules for you to follow, but I do trust that the One who has given us rules has done so for His glory and our good. My job is just to lay out the facts as I see them in Scripture and let you decide for yourself the best way to live in light of them. So let's take a look at three main biblical teachings about physical intimacy.

#1: God wants you to take sexual purity really seriously.

We've already glanced at one of the weightiest passages on purity, 1 Corinthians 6:18-20, but let's take another look:

> Run from sexual sin! No other sin so clearly affects the body as this one does. For sexual immorality is a sin against your own body. Don't you realize that your body is the temple of the Holy Spirit, who lives in you and was given to you by God? You do not belong to yourself, for God bought you with a high price. So you must honor God with your body.

The apostle Paul gives three reasons for sexual purity:

1. When you become physical with a guy before marriage, you're essentially hurting yourself.
2. The Holy Spirit lives in your body, and He doesn't take kindly to intruders.
3. God bought you with Jesus' blood, so your body doesn't belong to only you anymore.

You need to weigh your actions carefully. Any one of those three reasons could stand on its own, but *combined*? We have every reason to "run from sexual sin!"

There's another passage that really underscores the importance of sexual purity. First, a little background. Until Jesus came to earth, if non-Jews (Gentiles) wanted to follow God, they could. But they had to agree to adopt the many customs and practices of the Old Covenant that God had made with Abraham years and years before. We're talking all sorts of customs: circumcision, ritual purification, regulations about food and clothing, keeping the Sabbath, and so on.

Now fast-forward to circa AD 40. The good news about Jesus' resurrection had spread far and wide, and many Gentiles were coming to salvation. But because they lived in different cultures and were used to different customs and practices, not all of them were keeping the Jewish rules. In Acts 15, the apostles and elders (who were Jewish believers) got together to talk this over. Some thought the Gentile converts should keep all the Jewish rules. Others thought they should have to keep only some of them, such as circumcision. When all was said and done, they decided there were only three practices important enough to require of all the new Gentile believers. Guess what one of them was? Yep: sexual purity. (For the other two, you'll just have to read Acts 15! Note: They sound strange to us but made perfect sense to a Jewish culture.) Of all the hundreds of commands God had given His chosen people over the centuries, sexual purity ranks in His top three for you and me. He takes what we do with our bodies very seriously, and so should we.

#2: God wants you to be in charge of your body.

Because God is so passionate about your purity, it makes sense that He'd want your mind—not your hormones—to be in control of your body. Peter, who was taught by Jesus firsthand, says,

> Dear friends, I warn you as "temporary residents and foreigners" to keep away from worldly desires that wage war against your very souls. Be careful to live properly among your unbelieving neighbors. Then even if they accuse you of doing wrong, they will see your honorable behavior, and they will give honor to God when he judges the world. (1 PETER 2:11-12)

In other words, because you're really a citizen of heaven instead of earth, don't give in to the pressure you're facing to use your body for anything God wouldn't smile on. People are watching. They're either going to see a young woman so in love with God that she can't bring Him disgrace, or they're going to see a girl so in love with a guy that she can't say no to him. Which girl do you want to be?

Peter goes on to say,

> Exercise your freedom by serving God, not by breaking the rules. Treat everyone you meet with dignity. Love your spiritual family. Revere God. (1 PETER 2:16-17, MSG)

I love 1 Peter 2:16 because it leads back to two of my favorite things: freedom and family. We have tremendous freedom in Christ! But we do that freedom an injustice when we use it as an opportunity to sin. Treat your brothers like brothers, and insist that they treat you like a sister! When you cement yourself to a guy in the name of freedom, you're not doing yourself—or your guy—any favors. You're only setting yourself up to get crushed.

Physical intimacy before marriage is also a lot like quicksand.

Quicksand is dangerous for two reasons. One, it can look harmless. If you don't know what to look for, you'll step into it obliviously. Two, once you start sinking, it's incredibly hard to get free. That stuff is deadly. I'm sure you can see the parallel. I can't tell you how many girls I've talked with who had no idea how quickly a little "innocent" intimacy got out of control. And once they went there with a guy, the cycle seemed impossible to break. I know how they feel—I was one of those girls too.

Like quicksand, the danger of physical sin can be hard to spot. And like quicksand, once you're stuck, you're stuck good. That's why the apostle Paul was so adamant about not getting trapped in the first place! Remember 1 Corinthians 6:12?

> You say, "I am allowed to do anything"—but not everything is good for you. And even though "I am allowed to do anything," I must not become a slave to anything.

This verse holds the key to staying pure. Christ *died* for your freedom. You used to be a slave to sin, but He reversed all that when He died and rose again. Now His daughters are free to *stay free*. That means you have the power to say no to any physical intimacy that would trap you—that would cement you to a guy who isn't your husband.

I get really fired up when I talk about freedom. If you could see me right now, you'd think I had gone mad. I'm literally on the edge of my seat, typing on my laptop like I'm going for the Guinness record for most keys broken while writing a book. I care about your freedom *so* much! Let's be real for a minute. Can you think of any other sin we girls so easily fall into, and fall so *hard* into? Sure, we deal with lots of issues, from body image to family feuds. But there's a very real danger in getting *crushed* by physical sin. There's an innocence that's being lost among an entire generation of young women as they allow guys to lead them into an incredibly dangerous, self-destructive sin. As my husband, Paul, mentioned earlier, you can't trust that a guy is going to have your best interest in mind in the heat of a spicy moment. That's why God wants *you* to be in control of your body—not your crush, boyfriend, or even fiancé.

#3: God wants you to wait to awaken love.

A very wise woman (King Solomon's bride) strongly warned other young women "not to awaken love until the time is right" (Song of Solomon 3:5). What does it mean to "awaken love"? Some might disagree, but I don't think the answer is all mystical or anything. Because the book of Song of Solomon is very physical and talks a ton about sexual intimacy, I think the Shulamite woman (Mrs. Solomon) is simply warning us against getting turned on—against "awakening" our or our boyfriend's desire for sex. God made a natural progression for sex, and the first step is awakening love. In a practical sense, awakening love is doing anything with a guy that gets you to a place where your hormones kick in and you crave more. Once you get to that place, it's very difficult to stop—hence, the Shulamite's warning not to go there!

I love Song of Solomon because it reminds us that God isn't forbidding steamy, romantic sex forever. In case you've never heard, God is no prude! He created sex to be a sweet expression of commitment and oneness. When that experience is enjoyed between a husband and wife, there's nothing on earth quite like it. But without the marriage commitment, intimacy will end up doing more harm than good.

So there they are: God's rules for physical intimacy. What you do with them is up to you. You can either disregard them as old-fashioned advice for a bygone generation, or you can embrace them as timeless guidance for a girl who loves God.

A Case for Boundaries

Obviously, my hope is that you will embrace God's guidelines for physical intimacy so you can enjoy the freedom of a clear conscience and be blown away by God's blessings for your obedience. But can I be brutally honest for a minute? A lot—I mean *a lot*—of girls have promised God they were going to save themselves for marriage, and then . . . they *didn't*. They wanted to stay pure, planned on staying pure, vowed to stay pure, but then one day found themselves knee-deep in regret and shame over what they had done with a guy. So let me ask you this: What makes you different? How are you going to keep your commitment to purity when girls all around you are failing to?

I ask those questions not because I don't believe you can do it but because I know that in order to stick to your guns, you're going to need a healthy dose of humility. You're going to have to know you are *not* stronger than anyone else and sheer will-power isn't enough to keep you from stumbling. What will set you up for success is not the strength of your will in the heat of the moment but your ability to set firm, wise boundaries before you ever enter into a relationship.

In Proverbs 7, Solomon (super-wise man, remember) alludes to the importance of boundaries. He tells the story of a guy who basically walks right into physical temptation with a married woman and is toast before he knows what hit him. Solomon cautions that the way to keep away from physical sin is to let wisdom and insight protect you (see verses 4-5) and to keep from "wandering" toward danger in the first place (see verse 25). Very solid advice.

Boundaries are those wise lines of defense that protect you from yourself and from any guy who would put himself and his desires above your good. Boundaries keep you from wandering into danger. The quicksand nature of physical sin makes boundaries absolutely necessary for any girl who values her purity. You get to decide what boundaries are best for you personally, given your history, weaknesses, and strengths. I only ask that you give them some serious thought and prayer. Then, like Solomon advised, I'd encourage you to write them deep within your heart (see verse 3).

So, when you think about boundaries, what comes to mind? Here are some thoughts that other girls have shared with me:

"I won't have sex before marriage."
"I'm okay with kissing, but that's it."
"I won't let a guy put his hands under my clothes."
"I'll only hang out with a guy in a group but not
    one-on-one."
"Oral sex is okay because that's not technically sex."
"I won't be in the dark alone with a guy."
"If we've gotten turned on, then we've gone too far."
"I'll just tell him if he's doing anything I'm not okay with.
    I know he'll respect me and stop."

That's a pretty broad spectrum, right? Some of those boundaries are really helpful, and some are like trying to cage a hungry lion with string and a few Popsicle sticks! (Also, for the record, let me clarify that oral sex *is* sex. C'mon now—it's right there in the name!)

Like I said, *you* are responsible for deciding which boundaries are going to protect you from making mistakes you never want to make. If you need some more food for thought to help you decide where to draw your personal boundaries, let me give you two *challenges* to consider.

Love in the Light

I love light. Sunshine makes me giddy like few things in life can. I adore lying out in the sun—poolside, with a nice, icy *agua*. The Bible talks a lot about light and always in a positive sense. God has called us into His "wonderful light" (1 Peter 2:9), and Jesus called Himself "the light of the world" (John 8:12). Light can even help you fight the temptation of physical sin. Romans 13:12-13 says,

> Let us discard the deeds of darkness and put on the armor of light. Let us walk with decency, as in the daylight . . . not in sexual impurity and promiscuity. (HCSB; SEE ALSO JOHN 3:19-20; EPHESIANS 5:8-9)

Challenge #1: Use light like armor. When do people usually "stumble" into temptation? In the dark. I'm not saying people don't "get busy" during the day, but it's just not as much of a temptation. In the dark, with someone you're really attracted to—that's just a recipe for falling prey to "the deeds of darkness," right? Wisdom would say to use light to your advantage, because if you're intent on purity, darkness isn't going to help you in your quest. So how might light play a role in your personal boundaries?

A Daddy's Protection

Here's some more food for thought. God has given fathers a few important roles in their daughters' lives. According to God's plan for family, one of your dad's primary responsibilities is to guard your purity. Unfortunately, many dads have fallen short of living up to God's design for family life. If your dad isn't stepping up to fill that role—because he's not sure how to, or maybe because he's not sure you *want* him to—I am genuinely sorry, friend. If that's the case, the good news is that God also calls Himself your Daddy. He is happy to fill the role of protector of your purity. The problem is we haven't been in the habit of *letting* our dads—earthly dads *and* heavenly one—do their jobs. We get so intent on our independence that we buck against the very protection God designed for our good. It's time to change all that.

Challenge #2: Don't do anything with a guy that you wouldn't do in front of your dad (earthly father or heavenly one!). Seriously? Yeah, seriously. I know you're probably feeling squeamish right about now at the thought of doing anything in front of your dad! But that's the point, isn't it? There's something deep inside our hearts that tells us it would be wrong to do certain things with guys when our daddies are watching. That speaks to the truth of what I'm getting at here. Until your dad gives you away on your wedding day, let him do his job, and respect his role as protector even when he isn't watching.

Hope for the Broken

We've been talking an awful lot about the importance of purity and what tools will help you stay pure, but I'm well aware there's a good chance you've already experienced the flip side of the equation. I don't need to quote stats to you. They'd only confirm what you already know by experience: that way too many girls have already been burned by physical sin. And there's a good chance you're one of them.

To paraphrase 1 John 2:1-2, I've written this chapter so you won't be trapped by physical sin with a guy. But if you've already sinned—whether one time or hundreds of times—let me point you to Jesus, the One who died for your sins and is your advocate before the Father!

This is where the ink and paper you're holding in your hand seems so lacking. I wish you were sitting right here with me so I could look you in the eyes and tell you that you have *never* fallen too far for grace! The Bible is clear that if you confess your sin to God and turn back to Him, He will forgive you. Every. Single. Time. (See 1 John 1:9; Acts 3:19.) He wipes the slate clean. That doesn't mean you won't still suffer from the natural consequences of your sin (for example, emotional pain, memories of what went on, maybe being a mother before you're ready), but the *spiritual* consequences of your sin are removed "as far from [you] as the east is from the west" (Psalm 103:12).

Let's talk for a minute about the difference between shame and sorrow. If you've gone too far physically with a guy, I'm guessing you've probably experienced your fair share of shame. Shame is the painful emotion you feel when you know you're guilty of doing something really wrong. Shame is dark and imprisoning. Shame is for the guilty, but—here's the incredible part!—Christ took your guilt when He died on the cross. In God's eyes, you are no longer guilty. (How amazing is that?!) "Our guilty consciences have been sprinkled with Christ's blood to make us clean" (Hebrews 10:22). And if you are no longer guilty, then you no longer have reason to feel shame.

Sorrow over your sin, on the other hand, is both healthy and right. Paul explains the difference between godly sorrow and worldly sorrow (shame) in his second letter to the Corinthians:

> The kind of sorrow God wants us to experience leads us away from sin and results in salvation. There's no regret for that kind of sorrow. But worldly sorrow, which lacks repentance, results in spiritual death. (2 CORINTHIANS 7:10)

Did you catch that? God *wants* you to experience sorrow over your sin because it makes you not want to do it again! Paul continues,

> Just see what this godly sorrow produced in you! Such earnestness, such concern to clear yourselves, such indignation, such alarm. . . . You showed that you have done everything necessary to make things right. (VERSE 11)

Has sorrow over your sin made you dead set on not doing it again? Are you passionate about keeping yourself free from sin—passionate enough to either get married or end a relationship with someone you care deeply about? That's what godly sorrow should produce in your life—not guilt, but a zeal that won't rest until "you have done everything necessary to make things right."

Christ came for freedom—for *your* freedom! Be wise and stay free. Don't allow yourself to become a slave—either to sexual sin or to shame over that sin. Instead, embrace the hope that Christ came to give you, get fired up over your sin, and then let that godly sorrow produce holiness in your life.

Christmas Eve Doesn't Cut It

From a double rainbow against a dark sky to the undeniable pleasure in a scoop of chocolate gelato, our Daddy sure knows how to make us smile. He loves to give us good gifts! And, as the best gift-giver in the universe, He also knows the value of suspense. And I learned it too one Christmas.

'Twas the night before Christmas at the Jewett house, and everything was stirring . . . 'cause we got really excited about Christmas around our place. The stockings were hung, the lights were strung, and the presents were piled high under our decorated *tannenbaum*. Mom brought in our traditional Christmas Eve appetizer: sliced summer sausage, cheese, and *potica* (a Slovenian sweetbread), all sent with love from her family in Wisconsin. Everything was ready, and it was finally *time*.

Our family had a tradition of each opening one gift on Christmas Eve, and my sister and I had been eyeing the bounty of carefully wrapped packages for weeks, trying to decide which one we'd open first. We went around the circle, choosing one gift and opening it. And then, as we always did, we turned to Dad and begged, "Please can we open just one more? Pleeease?" I don't know why we asked. He had never given in, and there was no indication that this time would be different. But, contrary to all reason, this time he said yes!

In utter glee, we ran to the Christmas tree and chose another gift to open. Then, because the first attempt had worked, we tried again. "Please, Daddy? Just one more?" To our shock, he agreed again! So we went around, each choosing a gift and opening it. Certainly the fourth time wouldn't work, but we couldn't help but ask. And it was like the universe was coming undone—he said yes again . . . and again . . . and again . . . until all the presents were unwrapped, and we sat staring in disbelief at one another under a pile of wrapping paper. Had we really just opened *all* our presents on Christmas Eve? The absurdity of it had us feeling a little excited, elated even.

Then came Christmas morning.

In all my years of Christmases, that one stands out as the darkest, most depressing of all. There was no excited pitter-patter of feet down the hall to wake our parents before dawn. In fact, I think we all just slept in. There was nothing to get up for! The excitement of the night before was replaced by sheer and utter disappointment that Christmas morning, when there were no presents to open.

God knows a gift is better because of the wait. When we cheat the system by opening one of His perfect gifts before the right time, it ceases to be perfect. That's why the best gifts God gives us usually have a gift tag signed,

God has given us the amazing gift of sex, and He also knows the surprise on "Christmas morning" (the wedding night) will make the gift all the sweeter! If you don't give in by opening the gift on Christmas Eve, you won't be disappointed. I promise!

Daddy, thank You for giving me such good gifts! I know Your rules for romance and sex are for my good and for Your glory. Give me the strength I need to stand strong against temptation, and give me wisdom to know what kind of boundaries I need to set up in my life to guard my purity. I want to honor You and my future husband with my body. I love You. Amen.

Discussion Questions

1. *How is physical intimacy like cement? How is it like quicksand?*

2. *Before reading this chapter, where would you have drawn "the line" of physical intimacy? Have your views changed? How far back do you think you can stand and still "enjoy the view"?*

3. *Do you think a kiss is a big deal? Why or why not?*

4. *What guidelines has God given us for sex and all physical intimacy?*

5. *What do you think about the challenges to (1) use light like armor and (2) not do anything with a guy that you wouldn't do in front of your dad? Are they realistic? Would they help guard your purity?*

6. *Prayerfully consider what social and physical boundaries would be wise for you to set up in your life to protect your purity. Write them down in your journal.*

7. *What would you tell a friend who is crushed by going too far with a guy?*

8. *If you've given in to physical sin, how can "godly sorrow" fuel your present and future purity?*

CHAPTER 9

That Ever-Elusive Contentment

The last time I visited my sister, we took a hike near our childhood home. Alicia is twenty-five, tall, blonde, witty, self-sufficient, and single. As we picked our way down the mountain trail, between fallen logs and a bubbling stream, I asked her what she thinks it means to be content with singleness. She shot me one of her classic, sarcastic smiles and replied with a bit of a laugh, "Content? I'm *not* content to be single. I still rebel against the idea all the time!"

We both laughed out loud at her enthusiastic honesty. But after a few more silent paces down the trail, she added, "It's funny, though—you can definitely tell a difference between single girls who love God and those who don't."

Of course I wanted to hear more. "What do you mean?"

"It's about their focus on what their time being single is for—what the purpose is. The ones who aren't Christians view their singleness as all about them—like it's a time for them to do whatever they want, focus on their careers without being tied down, do whatever makes them happy, and just date and sleep around to figure out what *they* 'want.'"

"And the Christian girls?" I asked.

"For us, it's about serving. Being single is the time when you can really focus on helping others and serving God without distraction. It's a lot harder to do that when you're married and have kids and all of that—or so I hear."

I had to smile at that because she had, in fact, heard that from yours truly, maybe on more than one occasion. (One of the downsides to being my little sister is that Alicia has to endure the occasional mini sermon.)

I always appreciate my sister's honesty, and I know she's definitely not alone in her struggle to master contentment. I spent many years on the front line of that battle, and I know very few girls who would say they've figured it out. Contentment is ever-elusive and often misunderstood, but getting a handle on it is one of the keys to finding your guy without getting crushed. So let's take a look at what contentment is, what it isn't, why we have so much trouble with it, and how you can develop it in your own heart.

What Is Contentment?

I never had my own car in high school, but once I got my license, my parents were nice enough to let me drive their 1974 Dodge Dart Swinger on occasion. (I think they may have had ulterior motives, like my abject humiliation, maybe?) What can I say about the Swinger? It was the epitome of the disco mobile. Imagine a retro, olive green, extra-long hotdog on wheels, with a vinyl top and about a six-inch clearance, and you'll start to imagine my disgrace. The front bench seat's (yes, *bench*) springs had given up long before, so when I drove alone, I tilted to one side like a homie cruisin' the hood. And I'm pretty sure it had an 8-track for an audio system (you'll have to ask your grandparents what that is).

But here's the thing: It was a car. Never mind that it was hideous—it had wheels and it drove, and that meant freedom. The Swinger and I could go where we wanted, when we wanted, and with the windows down and my cool shades on, I could almost imagine I was driving my dream car. (Maybe that's pushing it a bit.) I was thankful to have my own ride. I wasn't ecstatic about it or anything, but I was *content* to drive that Dodge Dart because it did what it needed to do: get me places.

My good friend Abby was given a brand-new, chili pepper–red, smokin' hot Ford Mustang for her first car. It shone like a glass Christmas ornament and diffused that intoxicating, new-car smell. We loved to cruise around in that thing, windows down, cool shades on, music blasting, feeling like the crazy fiends we were not. It was a dream car.

Now let's say one day Abby had come to me and offered to swap the keys to our cars—she'd give me her Mustang in exchange for my Ghetto Mobile. Would I take the deal? Shoot-chyeah! And then I'd leave the country with my new, hot set of wheels before she could change her mind! I was *content* to drive my Swinger, but that doesn't mean I wouldn't have traded it for something dreamier if given the chance. There was nothing wrong with driving the Dodge (other than embarrassment), but if I had the option of a Mustang, of course I'd opt for that.

That's a reasonable view of contentment.

Contentment is being *satisfied* with your relationship status.

You probably won't ever be ecstatic, thrilled, or giddy about being single, but you *can* be satisfied. And it's okay to view a healthy, God-honoring relationship as a "trade up" and look forward to having that someday too.

Thinking back to Proverbs 27:7 (from chapter 2), you could also think of contentment as the feeling you have after a good meal. "A person who is full refuses honey, but even bitter food tastes sweet to the hungry." Remember my green grape debacle? Being satisfied with singleness means you're full enough to refuse those green grapes dropped on a trail (that is, any relationship that isn't best for you). That doesn't mean you wouldn't take a steak dinner after a long day of hiking (a godly man in God's perfect timing); you just won't settle for less than you deserve because you're desperate for love. A girl who's content waits to feast on the right guy at the right time instead of stuffing herself now with a cheap imitation of what she really wants just to satisfy her craving for love.

Singleness: God's Gym for Your Heart

Contentment keeps us from being tempted by second-rate infatuation, but it's important for another reason: It makes us strong and dependent on God.

Let's just go ahead and say it: Singleness can be a type of suffering! It doesn't just *feel* that way most days, it technically *is*. Elisabeth Elliot, the author of *Passion and Purity* and a woman I really respect, defines suffering as "having what you don't want, or wanting what you don't have."[11]

Is singleness something "you don't want"? Do you want "what you don't have"—like a *guy*? Granted, singleness is not nearly as dramatic as what we would usually call suffering, but I see it as the training grounds for trusting God and deferring our hopes and dreams to Him. And just like every other type of suffering, we can either kick and scream and throw a little hissy fit over what God has chosen for us, or we can embrace it, turn to God, and learn from the struggle.

Romans 5:3-5 says,

> We can rejoice, too, when we run into problems and trials, for we know that they help us develop endurance. And endurance develops strength of character, and character strengthens our confident hope of salvation. And this hope will not lead to disappointment. For we know how dearly God loves us, because he has given us the Holy Spirit to fill our hearts with his love.

If you'll let the Holy Spirit do His work, singleness can help you develop endurance and strength of character and can even strengthen the confidence you have in your salvation. But if you fight against singleness and do everything in your power to change your relationship status—even if that means breaking God's instructions for relationships—God's just going to have to teach you contentment some other way. Trust me, if you don't learn the secret to contentment now, in singleness, then you're going to have to learn it another way later (in a way that will probably be equally unpleasant!).

When your groom slides that wedding ring on your finger, you don't suddenly transform into a perfectly content bride. If you weren't content in singleness, you won't be satisfied when you're married, either. Oh, you might finally be okay with your relationship status, but will you be content not having other things that you really want later on? Maybe it's a house when you have to rent, a baby when your husband isn't ready, or a vacation that you just can't afford. The list of potential wants is endless. So choose your training ground: either work hard to learn contentment in singleness or keep having to learn the lesson over and over.

Because I learned to be content with driving the Dodge first, contentment with every car after that has been a piece of cake! Image how hard it would have been if I had started out driving a shiny, new Mustang and then had to learn how to be content to drive a beater car. The cool thing about learning to be satisfied with your lot while single is that it's like athletic training for your heart. Singleness is hard! Your heart gets all beefed up as you exercise your contentment muscles. Then, later on in life, your heart is strong enough to be content without other things you want. When your heart is strong, you can say with King David, "I will be satisfied with [God's] presence" (Psalm 17:15, HCSB), no matter what kind of suffering you face, and no matter what kind of want you don't have.

When you accept singleness as God's training ground for lifelong contentment, your solo status ceases to be a punishment and instead becomes a great gift. This verse from Isaiah so beautifully sums up what our attitude can and should be toward singleness:

> We're in no hurry, GOD. We're content to linger in the path sign-posted with your decisions. Who you are and what you've done are all we'll ever want. (26:8, MSG)

We're in no hurry. Take your time, God; we've got all the time in the world to stroll down this path of singleness (this path You've chosen for us) because who You are and what You've done is all we need. It's all we want. Whew! Can you say that to God today? Are you satisfied with singleness because you're satisfied in *Him*? I'm not suggesting you won't always desire to get married someday, but can you be content to linger with Him for *today*?

I absolutely love that verse, but it packs a punch, doesn't it? Why is it so stinking hard to be content in God alone?

Why Is Contentment So Hard?

I spent quite a bit of time asking myself that same question in my single years. If I love God and *want* to be content in Him alone, why can't I just do it? In retrospect, I think I've finally found a few answers to that question.

First off, the media gets all up in our heads. If you're begging God for contentment but then turn around and watch chick flicks, listen to romantic music, and read secular girls' magazines and romantic novels, well then, my dear, you're going to be fighting a losing battle! Don't underestimate the power the media wields on your relationship psyche. Of course we'll have a hard time being content with singleness if we're bombarding our minds with "perfect" relationships every day!

I also think we've turned Burger King's slogan into a life philosophy: We want everything our way, right away. We feel that we deserve happiness, and because we think having a boyfriend means happiness, we think we deserve a boyfriend. When we have that mind-set—that we should have whatever we want when we want it—we can be tempted to take verses like John 15:7 out of context:

If you remain in me and my words remain in you, you may ask for anything you want, and it will be granted!

God isn't our divine genie just waiting for us to ask so He can grant us our wishes. If we were actually remaining in Christ and letting His words remain in us, we would know the things we should ask for: not a boyfriend but gifts even *better* than that. Gifts like contentment!

But the main reason we have such a hard time with contentment goes back to the garden. Well, two gardens, actually: the Garden of Eden and a garden Charles Spurgeon once talked about. Here's what he said:

> Contentment in all states is not a natural propensity of man. Ill weeds grow apace; covetousness, discontent, and murmuring, are as natural to man as thorns are to the soil. You have no need to sow thistles and brambles; they come up naturally enough, because they are indigenous to earth, upon which rests the curse. . . . If we want flowers, there must be the garden, and all the gardener's care. Now, contentment is one of the flowers of heaven, and if we would have it, it must be cultivated. It will not grow in us by nature; it is the new nature alone that can produce it, and even then we must be specially careful and watchful that we maintain and cultivate the grace which God has sown in it.[12]

Let me sum that up: Contentment is hard because it's not natural! When I plant my garden each spring, I don't have to go out with a packet of weed seeds to get the weeds to grow. Somehow those little buggers are just always there. Weeds are the natural plants that grow in dirt. If I want flowers (or basil, or tomatoes, or snap peas, or lemon cucumbers) to grow in my garden, I have to intentionally plant the seeds, water them, and pull out the weeds that always spring up each year.

Because of our sin, the only plants that grow naturally in our hearts are weeds, and discontentment is high on the list of the most vigorously growing. If we want anything else to grow, we're going to have to enlist the help of our Divine Gardener.

My mother-in-law is bananas for roses. She has more than twenty-two varieties in her front yard, and when spring comes to her California home, it's like an explosion of perfume! You can smell her yard halfway down the block. And the colors? Bright yellow, tropical coral, powdery lavender, blood red . . . I could go on. When Charles Spurgeon describes contentment as "one of the flowers of heaven," I see Marilyn's roses, with all their beauty and fragrance. But they don't grow naturally. Not even close. She tends those puppies nine months out of the year, cutting them back for the winter, fertilizing, watering, even smashing the snails and beetles that threaten her master-pieces. When spring comes, she gets to enjoy fresh-cut bouquets around the house as well as the admiring praise of the neigh-bors. But her work doesn't stop then. She's out there all summer long, pruning, watering, and smashing more snails. She says that's the only way the roses will keep blooming late into the year. They need her continual care.

Isn't that the way of contentment? It's hard because it isn't natural. But it's also hard because it takes continual work and discipline! That's the part we don't like, right? God's strolling through our hearts with His big ole garden shears ready to prune the branches and dig up the weeds. A snip here, a whack there—sometimes we wonder if we'll survive! But remember, "if we want flowers, there must be the garden and all the gardener's care." Thankfully, our God is an expert gardener. He knows exactly what to cut back—exactly what discipline we need—in order to let the flowers of contentment flourish. Are you willing to let Him have complete control of your garden? Are you willing to discipline *yourself* to spend time in your garden, pruning, watering, fertilizing, and smashing the snails you find there?

How to Get Contentment

If you're ready and willing to start spending time in your own garden, cultivating contentment (your "flower from heaven"), let's get to work. Because contentment doesn't grow naturally in our hearts, it's something we have to learn how to do. Even the apostle Paul couldn't learn contentment the easy way (because there *isn't* one). He said,

> Not that I was ever in need, for I have *learned* how to
> be content with whatever I have. I know how to live
> on almost nothing or with everything. I have *learned*
> the secret of living in every situation, whether it is with
> a full stomach or empty, with plenty or little. For *I
> can do everything through Christ, who gives me strength.*
> (PHILIPPIANS 4:11-13, EMPHASIS ADDED)

You can do everything because Christ is your strength—Christ, who is all-powerful, all-knowing, all-good, and all-capable. The God who spoke the entire universe into being, holds it all together, and has beaten death? Yeah, I'm pretty sure

God can handle a little thing like teaching you contentment. But you have to give Him a chance! You have to do your part to turn to Him and believe He is able.

If contentment is something we have to learn, how can we get started? First, we have to give God permission to have free reign in our hearts, even if that means some serious (and painful) pruning. Once you've done that, follow these other practical tips to help you learn to be satisfied with the path God has chosen for you.

Change your mind.

Way back in chapter 1, we looked at the ties between our thoughts and our emotions, but we could all probably use a refresher. Remember Philippians 4:8-9?

> Fix your thoughts on what is true, and honorable, and right, and pure, and lovely, and admirable. Think about things that are excellent and worthy of praise. . . . Then the God of peace will be with you.

Our feelings—including feelings of loneliness and discontentment—come from the thoughts we think. If we let the weeds run wild in our thought life while we're single, we're going to be lonely, jealous, sad, and fearful of the future. But if we bust out the gardening gloves and start pulling those weeds up by the roots—by pinpointing the lies we believe and thinking true thoughts instead—our emotions and our lives will be so much healthier.

Remember that little thought chart we looked at in the first chapter? Here it is again, this time with specific thoughts we battle in singleness:

If I think . . .	Then I'll feel . . .
There must be something wrong with me because I don't have a boyfriend.	Doubt, self-loathing
I'd be happier if I were married.	Sadness, despair
I'm the only single girl on the planet.	Loneliness, isolation
I'll probably never get married.	Fear for the future
Why would God let *her* have a guy and not me?	Jealousy
I could meet my future husband today!	Hope
God desires my good and knows what's best for me. How amazing is that?	Joy
I don't have to be in a relationship to be complete. God is enough for me!	Peace, contentment

Remember, we're urged, "Let God transform you into a new person by changing the way you think. Then you will learn to know God's will for you, which is good and pleasing and perfect" (Romans 12:2). Part of learning contentment is letting God transform our way of thinking from relationship-centered thoughts to true, honorable, right, pure, lovely, and admirable thoughts. Contentment doesn't mean you'll be ecstatic or giddy about being single, and it certainly doesn't mean you won't feel a little lonely sometimes. But you won't be *ruled* by those emotions. You can stare loneliness in the face and know that God is at work creating roses.

Soak up Scripture.

God's words are more than just ink on paper. The words themselves are alive because they come from *the* Word, and they're able to do more than we can imagine. Hebrews 4:12 tells us,

> The word of God is alive and powerful. It is sharper
> than the sharpest two-edged sword, cutting between

soul and spirit, between joint and marrow. It exposes
our innermost thoughts and desires.

If you want to learn contentment, you *have* to get your
roots down deep and soak up the sweet nourishment of God's
Word. I really can't emphasize this enough. Consistently reading His words is like a daily vitamin that wards off loneliness
and despair:

> By means of their suffering, [God] rescues those who
> suffer. For he gets their attention through adversity.
> (JOB 36:15)

> Let all that I am wait quietly before God, for my hope
> is in him. (PSALM 62:5)

> A peaceful heart leads to a healthy body; jealousy is like
> cancer in the bones. (PROVERBS 14:30)

> Seek the Kingdom of God above all else, and live
> righteously, and he will give you everything you need.
> (MATTHEW 6:33)

> God will generously provide all you need. Then you
> will always have everything you need and plenty left
> over to share with others. (2 CORINTHIANS 9:8)

> True godliness with contentment is itself great wealth.
> (1 TIMOTHY 6:6)

I could go on and on listing verses that encourage, convict,
and turn our hearts toward God in the midst of singleness. The
best piece of advice I can give you if you want to learn contentment is to immerse yourself in God's Word.

Redirect your passion.

Look, if you're busy moping, you'll miss out on all the advantages of being single! And there are a lot. One of the biggest advantages you have by not having a significant other is freedom. You are free to try new things, venture to places you've never been, and make decisions for your future that don't hang on someone else's plans (like where to go to college or whether to do missions work). Plus, all that time you don't have to spend hanging out with (or on the phone with or texting with) a guy is time you can spend with God and your friends and discovering new passions.

So wipe those tears and find a hobby, missy. Pick up rock climbing, lacrosse, knitting, designing, creating fairy gardens, or collecting Chia Pets—whatever! Then read, reflect, take long walks, and savor each day you *get* to be single. It might not always be this way. There may come a time when you'll be (gladly) bound to another individual who needs you and wants to spend lots of time with you. And there may be a time when you're (gladly) a momma to a few little individuals who need you and want to spend lots and *lots* of time with you. And if you do it right, you'll look back on this season of singleness and be so glad you took full advantage of it.

You'll also be glad for this season of being solo if you find an outlet for all that healthy anticipation and excitement you have for your future. Redirect that passion you have for finding your guy and use this time to write love letters to your future husband. Tell him you're already praying for him and for you and for your life together. Tell him how excited you are to live your life beside him—loving, helping, serving, and following him.

And as you pen each letter, smile to yourself as you remember that God already knows exactly who you're addressing it to.

One more tip on redirecting your passion: Read books that teach a godly perspective on love, dating, and contentment. They're a great way to remind yourself how important contentment is and why it's worth waiting for your match. If you need ideas, you'll find a bunch of them on my Pinterest board titled "Favorite Books" (you can find the link at LifeLoveandGod .com).

Look outside yourself.

If you want to learn contentment, look outside yourself. Decide once and for all that you won't be the guest of honor at your own pity party. If you focus on your own misery, you'll miss opportunities to be a friend to others, do good, and represent Christ to your friends and family. Sometimes we just have to cut some windows in our selfishness and smell the fresh air outside! There's a whole world out there that needs the love of Christ you have to offer. You won't see the opportunities God has for you to help, love, and serve others if you're focused on your loneliness.

I say this with all the love in my heart as one who spent many years single: Let's get over ourselves! And then let's go out and see who else is hurting or lonely or in need of God's love. Help them, and you'll be helping yourself.

Free from Distraction

That day on the trail, my sister had it right: As a God-lover, singleness isn't about *me* and *my* time and *my* wants; it's a time of joy and freedom to serve God without distraction. It's a time to focus on God and on others. (Come to think of it, isn't that what our *whole* lives should be about?) Yes, it's a lecture Alicia has heard often, and now you've had to endure—I mean *you've been so very privileged* to hear—too. Let me sum it all up with a paraphrase of 1 Corinthians 7:29-38. (Paul spoke of marriage versus singleness, but the same principles apply to dating, too.)

Let me say this, my dear sister: The time we have on this earth is so short, and we never know when Christ may return. So from now on, those who are lonely shouldn't be absorbed by their loneliness or tears. And those with boyfriends should not focus on only their relationships or become too attached to them because everything in this life—except God—is temporary.

I want you to be free from the concerns of this life. A girl without a boyfriend can spend her time doing the Lord's work and thinking how to please Him. But a girlfriend is always preoccupied with earthly things, like how to please her boyfriend. Her interests are divided. Having a boyfriend is not a sin. But if a girl feels that God is asking her not to date, that's even better. So the girl who has a boyfriend does well, and the girl who doesn't have a boyfriend does even better.

I share all this because I love you, not because I'm some spinster who wants to pooh-pooh your parade. I want you to do whatever will help you serve the Lord best, with as few distractions as possible.

That's my prayer for you—that you'll serve the Lord with as few distractions as possible, whether single or taken. During our times of singleness, may we learn the fine art of contentment and be satisfied with God alone.

> *Father, oh how You know my desire to be married*
> *someday! If that is in line with Your will, prepare me*
> *in this season of singleness to be the best wife I can be*
> *by making me more like Your Son, Jesus Christ. And if*
> *marriage isn't Your perfect will for me, then still make me*
> *more like Jesus so I can bring You glory in my contentment.*
> *I trust You with my whole life, even with my heart. Amen.*

Discussion Questions

1. *What is contentment? What is contentment not?*

2. *If you are single now, would you say you've learned to be content?*

3. *How can singleness benefit you?*

4. If you don't learn to be content in singleness, how else might God teach you contentment?

5. If your heart is a garden, what steps do you need to take to cultivate your "flower from heaven" (contentment)?

6. What destructive thoughts about singleness do you struggle with? What truths can you think instead to help steer your emotions to a healthy place?

7. How does singleness enable you to serve God with fewer distractions?

8. If you're single today, are you taking full advantage of the benefits of your relationship status?

CHAPTER 10

Have a Vision
for an Extraordinary Love

I love home projects and power tools, and I've had a hankering to renovate an old home since . . . let's just say *a long time*. I'm pretty sure the obsession spawned from watching too many do-it-yourself shows on HGTV (Home and Garden Television). Anyway, a few years ago, I finally got the chance to indulge my pipe dream. The long-awaited project was a small, 1930s fixer-upper on the grounds of a church in the Pacific Northwest. Paul was the church's new worship pastor, and in exchange, they let us live in the house. The only catch? That quaint little house had been the residence of a rotating list of bachelors for more than ten years before we showed up.

To say the place had been neglected would be a horrendous understatement. To give you a little taste of how bad the condition was, consider exhibit A: the bathtub. When I first saw the bathtub, I thought the porcelain finish had been chipped away in a few places. But when I looked a little closer—I'm not making this up—it was the thick layer of grime buildup that had been chipped away, revealing little glimpses of the real tub underneath. I honestly don't think a single resident had scrubbed that bathtub in more than a decade. It was *that* gross. And the rest of the house followed suit. The carpets were stained, the living room had been splatter painted (yes, *splatter* painted) by the church youth group (in rainbow colors no less), and the cabinets smelled of mildew. There were holes in the walls and ants in the kitchen. Oh, and there was still a cache of bachelor food in the mint-green refrigerator (you can imagine how *that* smelled after stewing in there for ages). I took one look at that little house and I about freaked. What in the world was I thinking when we agreed to take that on?

Luckily, I'm a hopeless optimist, and in the month before we were to officially move in, I began to catch a vision. Something tripped inside me, and I started to consider the potential. Have you ever been so excited about something that you just couldn't sleep at night? That was me. I'd lie awake, wheels spinning, trying to come up with solutions for each of the home's— ahem—*potential* charming points. Sometimes I'd wake up at three in the morning with some epiphany and then shake Paul awake and make him listen to my newest idea for the bathroom or a solution for the kitchen cabinets. As I thought about each room—one at a time, top to bottom—I envisioned what I wanted that house to look like when all was said and done. And let me tell you, what I saw was *chic*.

After a month of planning, the time came for us to roll up our sleeves and get to work. For six weeks straight, we spent every single day working on that house. From morning till night, we scrubbed and we fixed, we painted and we tiled. We pulled up carpet and sanded wood floors. Men from the church came over and gutted the bathroom (hallelujah!). We worked on everything from the attic to the front yard, and at the end of our labor, not only did we have a place to live, but that little house looked even better than I had pictured it.

The secret? I had a vision. I could picture how I wanted that house to look, so every decision I made, from paint colors to curtain length, fell in line with my end goal. The blood, sweat, and tears (and I mean each of those quite literally!) were worth it because I knew we would be the happy beneficiaries of our hard work.

We've spent a lot of time together, you and I, talking about the ways you can navigate love without getting your heart crushed. Now comes the fun part! You get to dream and imagine and get excited about what happily ever after might look like in your own life. I want you to have a vision of what a beautiful, God-centered love story can be. Why? Because—just like my little house reno—if you know what you want your ever-after to look like, that vision is going to guide the decisions you make today and tomorrow and five years from now. Let's be real—if you want to be married to some trashy guy who beats on you and whose idea of a dream home is a run-down shack in the boondocks, you won't have any trouble getting there! A few poor choices and you're good to go.

But if you have a different idea about your future? If you want to marry a man who is going to cherish you and care for you and wants to build a life together with Christ at the center, you're going to have to know what you're looking for. This is why having a vision is so important: Your vision will determine your decisions. If you have a healthy vision, then your decisions—from whom you'll date to how you'll do it—will bring you closer to the end goal. But if you don't have a vision (or if that vision is distorted), every decision you make will lead you further away from God's ideal for your life.

Don't Stress the Details

I'm going to pause right here and make a distinction. When I talk about having a vision for your future life, I am not talking about the power of positive thinking! You might be able to close your eyes and picture with perfect clarity living in a mansion in the Bahamas with your Hollywood crush, but that doesn't mean it's going to happen. The idea of thinking something into existence is nonsense (and takes God completely out of the equation). When I talk about having a vision, I mean having a general idea about what you're waiting for, based on what you already know about God from the Bible.

If God knows marriage is what's best for you—best for His glory and your sanctification—then you already know He wants to be the center of your marriage. You know He wants you to submit to your husband and for your husband to love you as Christ loves the church (see Ephesians 5:21-25). If you have children someday, you know that God will want you to raise them to know Him (see Deuteronomy 6:4-9) and to discipline them in love (see Proverbs 13:24). You know you'll be happiest not if you're wealthy but if your home is marked by love (see Proverbs 15:17). And you can be sure that if you two are seeking God first, He will take care of everything else you need (see Matthew 6:33). These are the kinds of truths you already know God wants for you. We could call that God's "revealed will" for your life.

A wise girl develops a vision of what God's revealed will for her might look like in the real world. She considers what kind of man, lifestyle, and pursuits are in line with God's will for her. She searches Scripture so she knows what biblical principles should mark her life, and she watches people around her to see how the principles for waiting, dating, engagement, and marriage play out well. A wise girl gets excited about her future, knowing that the God of the Universe loves to give good gifts to His children! "Whatever is good and perfect" comes from Him (see James 1:17).

We girls are notorious for planning everything, from what we're going to wear to our future wedding to how we're going to get that cute guy to notice us. (I met a girl once who started a bridal binder at the age of fifteen. By the time I met her in college, it was a massive three-ring binder stuffed with dozens of pictures, invitation ideas, fabric swatches, and honeymoon brochures. How's that for planning ahead?) But a vision for your love life should be made up of generalities. You'll set yourself up for disappointment if you set your heart on particulars (exactly whom you're going to marry, what city you're going to live in, how old you want to be when "the one" comes along). God is sovereign; you are not. Daydreaming about the details will get you in trouble, but having a broad vision for your life is wise. Don't stress the details! Leave room for God's love of surprise and for the fact that He knows you way better than you know yourself. Have a vision for the broad strokes of a healthy love story, but leave the fine points for your heavenly matchmaker to decide.

Watch and Learn

If a wise girl watches the people around her to help her form her vision, just whom should she be watching? There's definitely something to be learned from watching people do love the *wrong* way (you know, learning from others' mistakes and all that), but the best tutors are those who show you how to do things right. The writer of Hebrews instructs us,

> Remember your leaders who taught you the word of God. Think of all the good that has come from their lives, and follow the example of their faith. (13:7)

A few thoughts on this verse: First, it assumes you have people in your life who are teaching you the Word of God (hint: that means you should!). Those people might include a pastor, a mentor, a parent, a teacher, or an older friend. Having someone you can actually see and talk with face-to-face is always best, but if you aren't surrounded by godly leaders, take advantage of all the great Christian books and websites out there that can help you on your journey. (You can find some good ones listed at LifeLoveandGod.com.) The second thing we learn in Hebrews 13:7 is that we should be watching the good coming from our leaders' lives. That command leaves room for an important truth: Not everything coming from their lives will be good! We are *all* sinners saved by grace, and the mentors in your life will have their share of "issues" too. So watch carefully. Imitate the good, and learn better from the bad. The last part of the verse builds on that thought: "Follow the example of their faith." As you see examples of men and women doing love and marriage right, add those pictures to a mental "vision scrapbook" and then follow in their footsteps.

I can't help but smile right now as I think about the men and women in my life who contributed snapshots to my own personal "vision scrapbook": my mom, Bobbie Griffin, Ron and Traci Harris, Preston and Chris Sprinkle, and authors such as Elisabeth Elliot, John Piper, and Eric and Leslie Ludy. At different times and seasons of my life, God brought women across my path who defined womanhood for me, couples who showed me what true love should look like, and families who shone with their peace, grace, and Christlikeness. The people who influenced my vision were all people I looked up to in different ways. Some of them were cool, others rather quirky, in a godly sort of way. Some took me under their wing without me even asking, others I had to pursue. (Some I sort of stalked incognito—shh!) Each snapshot was different, but they shared a common denominator: They loved God and were living out His principles in flesh and blood. *Those* are the people you want to be looking for.

It's human nature to try to imitate those you look up to. (If you have older brothers or sisters, you know what I'm talking about, right?) That's why it's so important to be enamored with the right influences and to distance yourself from the wrong ones. But let's talk for a minute about some influences you might not even realize are forming your vision. Are the books you read, the music you listen to, and the movies and shows you watch helping you cast a vision for a God-centered love story? Are they healthy influences? I don't want you to underestimate the influence your media choices have on the outcome of your life. Please consider this with me. If the bulk of your entertainment diet consists of media that twists God's truth and creates unhealthy expectations, if you're feasting on that instead of on God's truth, then your vision is going to be distorted. And if your vision is distorted, then every decision you make is going to get you one step closer to that distortion and one step further from God's ideal for your life. I can't emphasize this enough! Surround yourself with *good* examples of love—with beautiful pictures of godly romance—because you'll become what you admire.

Speaking of beautiful pictures, I have one for you to add to your collection. I've been dying to tell you this story since page 1! This is the story of Faith and Adam Kelly, a couple Paul and I have grown to respect and admire. Their story is such a sweet example of how a little unconventional thinking, coupled with two hearts set on honoring God, can turn a common love story into a thing of legends.

An "Old-Fashioned" Love

Faith is an all-American girl. She not only looks the part, with her gorgeous frame and long blonde hair, but she's also got more talent in her pinky finger than I'll ever have. I mean, come on now, the girl speaks five languages, plays the piano and sings, could whip up a ball gown on her sewing machine, and can run out on the field and contend with most guys I know at a game of football. More important, Faith has an incredible love for God. The first time I met Faith, she had just returned home after working for eight and a half years with her family at an orphanage in Cambodia. Yeah, let's just say Faith is the kind of catch that would make most guys delirious. (She would never admit to that, but because I'm telling the story, I'm just going to say it like it is.) Faith wasn't desperate for love, but the way she went about finding it at first left her broken and confused.

As a girl, Faith dreamed of meeting her future husband at a young age, growing up together, becoming best friends, falling in love, and getting married right out of high school (a lot like her own mom's story). She wanted that dream so badly that she held on to it tightly—*too* tightly—for a long time. Her parents believed that God would bring the right man to Faith in the right time, and they had a no-dating rule in the meantime. But as a tomboy, Faith had a lot of guy friends. Even though she couldn't "date" them, she reasoned, her parents certainly couldn't keep her from scoping the field of guy friends. They also couldn't stop her from forming emotional attachments to the best candidates.

When high school graduation came and went, with no man of her dreams in sight, Faith decided it was time to take matters into her own hands. Her parents' no-dating rule obviously wasn't working out for her, so she started dating behind their backs. It took a disastrous relationship (with a guy seven years older than her, previously married and an emotional train wreck) to help her come to her senses. She says that was a big turning point for her. "I began to see from experience that my parents knew what they were talking about! My mind was made up: I wanted to do it the 'old-fashioned way.'"[13]

Faith had heard about courting from reading books like the LITTLE HOUSE ON THE PRAIRIE series and *Little Women* as a kid. It seemed so romantic to have a man pursue you and to let a romantic relationship develop slowly, saving the physical relationship until marriage. But in the modern world, she felt there was only a slim chance of that happening. So when Adam came around, asking Faith's dad if he could court her with the intention of marrying her, Faith says she had to pinch herself to make sure it was really happening. And as their relationship unfolded, the two proved that sometimes the old-fashioned ways create the best modern love stories.

Faith met Adam while she was back in the States for a time.

Just two weeks after they met, she returned to Cambodia to continue working at the Cosette's Hope Children's Home. Over the course of a year and a half, they fell in love—8,954 miles apart. One of the blessings of being separated by an entire ocean was that they got to know each other without the distraction of physical attraction. They talked. They e-mailed. They wrote letters. But they didn't get too intimate, not even in their conversations. Faith got to know Adam for who he was, and he had to prove his devotion to her over time—a *long* time! Adam's willingness to pursue her on the other side of the world showed how serious he was about making her his wife and made him treasure her even more.

I had the privilege of watching Faith the day she became Mrs. Kelly. My oldest daughter, Ryan, attended the wedding with me. She was only four years old at the time, but her eyes were wide and I could sense her awestruck wonder as she watched Faith walk, gleaming, down the aisle. Ryan looked up at me with her big, brown eyes and whispered, "Mommy, I can't stop looking at her. She's so beautiful!" I had to agree. Every bride is a wonder to behold, but there is a whole other level of beauty to a bride who walks down the aisle in purity. I could almost feel the joy, anticipation, and freedom in the room as Adam took Faith to be his wife and kissed her—for the first time!

The thing I love most about Faith and Adam's story is that it's a story for each of us. Faith is such a great example of the power of second chances. Like me, and maybe like you, even though she was crushed—physically and emotionally—in past relationships, she left all that behind and chose a better way to find the love of her life. Her story proves that it's never too late to walk in purity.

Their story is universal in the sense that you could apply the principles and boundaries Faith and Adam used to any relationship. Here are some things about their experience to consider as you cast a vision for your own love story:

- *Their goal was marriage.* From day one, they had marriage in mind. No, they didn't know for sure if that's where God would take them, but they realized that the point of their relationship was to find out. They were trying to determine if they were compatible—not physically, but emotionally and spiritually.

- *They didn't isolate themselves.* Once they lived in the same country, Adam and Faith spent most of their time together surrounded by family and friends who loved them and helped keep them accountable to the boundaries they had set. Not dating one-on-one allowed them to get to know each other without the physical temptation of being alone.

- *They had boundaries.* Their firm boundaries allowed them to walk in purity until their wedding day. Faith says their solid stance on physical intimacy didn't make them feel deprived; instead, it created "an excitement and mystery leading up to our wedding day that was amazing!"

- *They both had peace about their relationship.* In past relationships, Faith had always been faced with red flags that made her question whether the relationship was right for her. But with Adam, there was no second-guessing. She was sure she was walking in God's will. "God opened every door and gave everyone involved a peace. That is when I knew—when I didn't feel the need to ask God, 'Is this okay?' Holding out for that peace was one of the hardest but most rewarding things I've ever done!"

When I asked Faith what advice she would give other girls who want to find their Mr. (Im)Perfect without getting their hearts crushed in the process, she zeroed in on purity:

I know from experience that keeping your purity is a hard task. Don't give in, and don't give up! Never compromise just because you think he's "the one." If he isn't, then you won't have any regrets, and if he is, then the physical stuff can wait for marriage (and it is so much better then!). So respect yourself and your own body. You are Christ's beautiful creation and bride! If you view yourself that way, you will have a newfound respect for yourself. You don't have to dress or act immodestly to get his attention or affection. In fact, he'll love and respect you more by seeing that you respect yourself and respect him by not causing him to stumble.

Why is purity at the top of her list for a perfect love story? Because she knows the devastation that comes if it's not:

In the "normal" dating routine, it's way too easy to give so much of yourself—emotionally, physically, and mentally—to a guy that when you do find "the one," you feel that there's only so much left for him. Some memories can't be erased, and even now that I'm married, sometimes feelings arise that can affect my relationship and closeness with Adam. I see now that

I robbed us of what was rightfully ours as a married couple.

Sobering realities, right? That's why having a vision of what you want your love story to look like is so important! If you know you want to save every piece of your body and heart for your future husband, you're going to run the other direction from any guy who tries to rob you of those things today, whether he "loves" you or not. And if you've already given too much of yourself away, having a renewed vision can help you redeem what was lost. You can still have a beautiful, *pure* love story no matter what your past experiences may be.

Faith and Adam's story is just one picture to add to your vision scrapbook. I don't expect that your relationship will look exactly like theirs, just as my and Paul's love story is a romance all its own. My prayer is simply that one day your own love story will also inspire others to walk in purity.

When Dreams Come True

I love this passage from Proverbs that we looked at in chapter 4. This is one of those verses you need to write down somewhere you'll see it often.

> Hope deferred makes the heart sick,
>   but a dream fulfilled is a tree of life. . . .
>
> It is pleasant to see dreams come true.
>   (PROVERBS 13:12,19)

I'm all about hard truths, and the hard truth about relationships is that even if you play the game right, you're going to have your share of heartsickness before you find your match. You're going to feel the pangs of loneliness. You're going to question whether God is ever going to bring you a husband. You're going to cry your share of tears, feel the sting of rejection, and have to make decisions that tear your heart up. But the beautiful promise of this verse is that "hope deferred"—all that waiting for the dream—only sweetens its arrival. When dreams finally come true and God brings you face-to-face with the man you've been waiting for (or face-to-face with your heavenly Groom, if you don't get married in this life), the joy will be . . . I can't even describe it! It's *that* good.

Are you willing to wait for the dream? There are plenty of people out there who will tell you it's not worth the wait. They'll say that you can have intimate relationships outside of marriage and not miss out on anything and your heart will be just fine. Obviously, that's not working out very well for us as a society. Girls are getting crushed in record numbers. But *you* don't have to be one of them. Have a vision. Hold on to your dream—the dream of a God-honoring, fulfilling, and beautiful romance. If you do, I can't promise you'll get married, but I can promise you will not be disappointed!

When your dream does come true, the task doesn't end there. Maintaining a God-honoring, fulfilling, and beautiful romance is a lot of work! Perhaps that's another book for another day. I want to challenge you with one caution, though, that applies to your "happily ever after." Even once you think you've found the man you'll spend the rest of your life with, don't forget God. Once dreams come true, He is just as vital to your life as ever. That's exactly what God told the Israelites once. Here's my rough paraphrase of Deuteronomy 8:11-20:

Once dreams come true, be even more careful not to forget God. Once you've found the man of your dreams and you're reveling in the newfound joys of love, once he proposes and you've gotten married, and once you are building a happy life together, be careful! Don't forget God! He walked with you through the lonely times, He taught you and disciplined you when you messed up, and He showed you that He is enough for you. God took you through those difficult roads to teach you to rely on Him for your own good! He made you wait for your dream so you would never say to yourself, *I've achieved this great relationship with my own strength and energy.* Remember God! He is the one who allows your relationship to thrive so that He will be glorified. But if you forget God once your dreams have come true and you have what you want—if you start chasing after things other than God— then you'll reap the consequences.

I give you that challenge because I know how quickly a heart feasting on God can turn right around and become completely preoccupied with a guy—even a really great one! No matter how long you wait for your marriage partner, remember that your whole life (from your first breath to your dying day) should revolve around God. He must be your first love if you're going to enjoy the life He wants for you. Then you can say with Isaiah,

I am overwhelmed with joy in the LORD my God!
For he has dressed me with the clothing of salvation
and draped me in a robe of righteousness. I am like
a bridegroom in his wedding suit or a bride with her
jewels. (61:10)

There is a jaw-dropping beauty about God-obsession—about a girl who is clothed in her salvation like a designer wedding dress. (On the flip side, boy-obsession is like wearing a muumuu to your big day.) My prayer for you is that you will wear your "dress" of salvation well and be overwhelmed with joy in God as you wait for your own love story to unfold.

Daddy, I'm so anxious for the day when You will "give me away" to the man You've already picked out for me! But until then, help me to form a healthy vision for what a God-honoring romance can look like and to make wise decisions that will get me closer to that reality. I know it won't be easy to wait; please help me to wait well! I want to bring You glory in every aspect of my life, including my love life. I adore You, God, and I am so thankful to be Yours! Amen.

Discussion Questions

1. Describe the relationship between your vision and your decisions.

2. Who has contributed snapshots to your "vision scrapbook"? Who or what is influencing your vision for your future today?

3. *Pull out your journal one last time. Spend a few minutes describing the kind of relationship you want to have someday. What kind of guy do you want to marry? What do you hope your family life will be like?*

4. *Think about some of the big decisions you've made in life. Now that you've thought about the kind of love story you want to have, were your big decisions wise decisions?*

5. *What choices do you know you'll need to make if you're going to have a shot at getting to your dreams for romance?*

6. *Do you think it's possible to have a beautiful vision for life that doesn't include an earthly romance?*

7. *Do you find it hard to trust God with the details of your life, like how long you'll be single and whether you'll ever get married? Why or why not?*

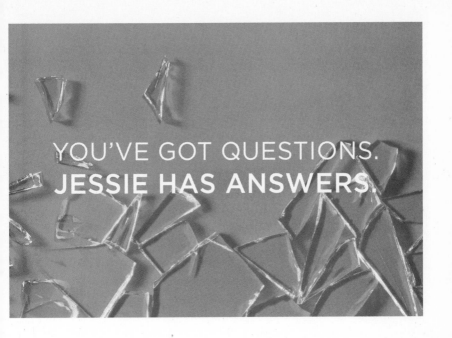

Notes

CHAPTER 1: THOSE BLASTED BUTTERFLIES

1 *Merriam-Webster's Collegiate Dictionary*, 11th ed., s.v. "crush."

2 Every woman, because she is a woman, has a built-in beauty about her. I wish I could go into it more here, but for now you're just going to have to trust me!

CHAPTER 2: HE CAN'T MAKE YOU WHOLE

3 This paragraph is compiled from the truths found in verses such as John 3:16, Isaiah 62:4-5, Ephesians 5:21-33, Psalm 139, Isaiah 43:7, and Zephaniah 3:17.

4 If you want to know more about what it means to have a relationship with God and where to start, visit the "Deeper" page at www.LifeLoveAndGod .com.

CHAPTER 4: HE CAN'T BREAK YOU

5 The names and some details in this story have been changed to protect the individuals' privacy.

6 My paraphrase of Matthew 7:24-27.

CHAPTER 5: IS THERE A BETTER WAY? (TO DATE OR NOT TO DATE?)

7 The time when your parents technically stop being your "authority" is under debate. Some feel it's after you get married; others think it's once you're not living under their roof anymore. I'm not here to argue for the letter of the law but rather its intent. I'd challenge you to honor and obey your parents even if you have moved out and don't think you're under their "jurisdiction" anymore. Remember, God didn't put a limit on the promise either—it's for a long and prosperous life!

CHAPTER 7: BECOMING MISS (IM)PERFECT

8 Jonathan Miles, "11 Reasons Men Love Women," *Fox News*, May 4, 2013, http://www.foxnews.com/health/2013/05/04/11-reasons-men-love-women /?intcmp=features#ixzz2TBzfCHm8, accessed May 13, 2013.

9 Classy doesn't have to mean old or snobbish. For some fun, modern takes on classy clothes, check out the Life, Love and God Pinterest board titled "Cute (& Modest) Clothes": http://pinterest.com/lifeloveandgod/cute -modest-clothes/.

CHAPTER 8: RESPECT THE FIRE AND YOU WON'T GET BURNED
10 For one source from a Christian perspective, see Dannah Gresh, *What Are You Waiting For?* (Colorado Springs, CO: WaterBrook, 2011), 40–44.

CHAPTER 9: THAT EVER-ELUSIVE CONTENTMENT
11 Elisabeth Elliot, *A Path Through Suffering* (Ventura, CA: Regal, 1990), 56.
12 Charles Spurgeon, "Sermon No. 320," March 25, 1860, at New Park Street Chapel, Southwark, reprinted at "The New Park Street Pulpit," http://www.spurgeon.org/sermons/0320.htm, accessed April 23, 2013.

CHAPTER 10: HAVE A VISION FOR AN EXTRAORDINARY LOVE
13 E-mail interview with Faith on June 18, 2013. Used with permission.